The Duping
of America

The Duping of America

HOW WE HAVE BEEN DECEIVED INTO THINKING ABORTION IS ACCEPTABLE, AND THE SCIENTIFIC, LEGAL, MORAL AND PHILO-SOPHICAL PROOF THAT IT IS NOT.

Rick Garrett, M.A. M.Ed.

Liberty Hill
Publishing

Liberty Hill Press
2301 Lucien Way #415
Maitland, FL 32751
407.339.4217
www.libertyhillpublishing.com

Unless otherwise indicated, Scripture quotations taken from the New
American Bible Revised Edition (NABRE). Copyright © 2010, 1991,
1986, 1970 Confraternity of Christian Doctrine, Inc., Washington, DC
All Rights Reserved.

Printed in the United States of America.

ISBN-13: 978-1-6322-1247-4
Ebook: 978-1-6322-1248-1

To the millions of innocents who have lost their lives and to those who work tirelessly for the truth.

"Our lives begin to end the day we become silent about things that matter." – Dr. Martin Luther King, Jr.

Table of Contents

Chapter 1 – Introduction

A lie doesn't become truth, wrong doesn't become right, and evil doesn't become good just because it's accepted by a majority. – Booker T. Washington

According to most statistical sources, approximately 3,000 lives were lost today in the United States.[1-3] Approximately the same number will be lost tomorrow, the next day and the next. These lives have not been lost to cancer or other diseases, car accidents, drug overdoses, or war. These lives have been lost at the hands of individuals who felt they were too inconvenient to live. Worse yet, a small segment of our society convinced us that there is nothing wrong with this, and our legal system sanctioned it. It sounds like the script for a science fiction horror movie. But we have been duped into believing abortion is acceptable.

The Guttmacher Institute, Planned Parenthood's former research and policy analysis organization, states that more than 60 million abortions have been performed in the United States since it became legal in 1973.[2] If the number of abortions performed per day is spread out over the 24 hours in that day, in the time it takes you to read this page, almost three innocent, unborn human beings will be killed.

The magnitude of this number is staggering. According to the U.S. Department of Veteran Affairs, this is over fifty times the number of U.S. soldiers who have died in battle in all wars fought by the United States.[4] American Cancer Society figures indicate that the number of human lives lost to abortion in 2011 is almost double the number of people in the U.S. who died of cancer that same year.[5] The total number of abortions performed to date in the U.S. alone is more than the **combined** populations of Switzerland, Denmark, Finland, Austria, Sweden, Greece, New Zealand and Norway. In fact, the United States has the highest abortion rate in the western world, and the third-highest abortion rate of all developed nations worldwide.[6] Our abortion laws and policies are more liberal than any in western Europe, and are in the same category as China's and North Korea's. How did this happen?

Chapter 2–A New Language

The right word fitly spoken is a precious rarity. –
John Boyle O'Reilly

I n a later chapter, the media's role in paving the way for a more liberal agenda in the U.S. will be examined in more detail, but a good place to begin is by uncovering the carefully chosen language regarding abortion they helped create and promote.

As Alexandra Desanctis from the National Review notes,

> Refashioning the meaning of words to fit political purposes is in vogue. This is perhaps nowhere more apparent than when proponents of "the right to choose" insist that "women's autonomy" is protected by the "constitutional right to privacy" because of the "intimate nature of personal health-care decisions."[7]

Obianuju Ekeocha, the author of "Target Africa–Ideological Neocolonialism in the Twenty-First Century writes

> New language was developed by feminist activists to rationalize the killing of the unborn. New phrases such as "blob of tissue", "right to choose", "reproductive justice", "right to privacy",

3

and "bodily autonomy" were created to gloss
over the reality that abortion kills an innocent
human being.[8]

When we hear anti-life advocates talk about "reproductive rights" or "reproductive health," make no mistake, behind these antiseptic euphemisms, what they are actually referring to is nothing more than abortion. To make the concept of abortion more palatable, abortion advocates have created this new jargon to sanitize the idea of tearing a preborn child limb from torso from her mother's womb. They also say things like "she decided a child would interfere with her career at this point, so she decided to *terminate*."

In the last few decades, the words "values" and "morals" have become taboo in public discourse. Another new combination of words became popular: "whatever is right for you." In this era of sanctioning "whatever is right for you," these words contrast with the fact that at one time, universal truths, however inconvenient, did exist. These five words, in some cases, encouraged individuals to worship at the altar of their own comfort and convenience, regardless of the consequences.

It is interesting how abortion proponents loosely use the term "The right to choose," but never seem to finish the sentence. The right to choose what? The right to choose to decapitate and dismember an innocent human life because it is too inconvenient for his parents' lifestyle? More than 90% of abortions are done on healthy babies for matters of convenience.

Political commentator, author, lawyer, and public speaker Ben Shapiro sums it up best:

> No more euphemisms. Let's call it what it is. No
> one has the right to kill a baby. Stab a baby through
> the chest, and we call it murder. Dismember and

decapitate a fully formed baby in utero and it's a right. The baby's right to life is more important than your convenience. You don't get to choose another human being's death. Do you think this is a life or not? If you don't think it's a life, you'll probably do whatever you want with it. If you think it's a life, you can't do anything with it. It's actually a very simple issue–it's either a life or it isn't. It's nasty, cruel and degrading, this idea that you get to decide whether something is a life or not based on whether it's convenient. Who uses euphemisms? Those who don't have a valid argument. It's always 'terminate a pregnancy, right to choose', instead of 'I'm going to have my baby dismembered and decapitated today.'[9]

After the passage of Roe v. Wade in 1973, those who advocated abortion on demand were labeled "PRO choice" and favored abortion "rights" and "reproductive freedom." The words "pro" and "choice," as defined in the dictionary as well as in common usage, carry definite positive connotations. "Rights" and "freedom" are terms even more closely tied to a positive context and have even patriotic overtones. It just naturally followed in the minds of many Americans that the "right" to terminate a pregnancy was part of the group of rights that included the right to vote, to bear arms, a right to a trial by one's peers, etc. The "right to *life*, liberty, and the pursuit of happiness," however, was overlooked.

Those who questioned Roe vs. Wade were also labeled by the press, but with less glowing terms: "ANTI abortion rights" groups ("anti" having as much a negative connotation as "pro" a positive one). The press cast them in the light of having the audacity to oppose recently discovered political and social "rights." They painted them as angry, negative people (ironically just what those who support abortion usually are). In the process, they conveniently glossed over the medical fact, as we will also see in another chapter, that the unborn are individuals with their own unique DNA and a beating heart, but deserved no rights of their own, not even the basic right to life.

Let us suppose for a minute that the press had a pro-life slant. Those who favor protecting the unborn would be called "pro-life" or "right to life" supporters. "Pro-choice" advocates might now be called "anti-life" or "pro-death" proponents. If these terms sound odd, consider when was the last time you heard them, if at all. This is the extent to which the press shapes public opinion.

There is perhaps no greater manipulation of language in this debate than the "Freedom of Choice Act," carefully crafted by liberal politicians. It was introduced in the House and Senate in 2004, after earlier versions were introduced but not enacted in 1989 and 1993. Its purpose was to prohibit federal, state and local governments from interfering with a woman's "right" to abort her child.

Just consider the title alone: "Freedom." Again, there is probably no other term in the English language infused with as much patriotism, inalienable human rights, and the democratic principles upon which our country was founded. What's more, combine "freedom" with "choice" and you have a concept that on the surface, appears to be something that should be enjoyed by every American. Actually, nothing could be further from the truth. Behind this very astute and deceptive use of words is the "choice" and "freedom" to end millions of innocent human lives.

Anyone, including those who support the lives of the unborn, but who are still using the term "pro (or anti) *abortion rights*" are reinforcing the idea that abortion is a fundamental human right. Instead, we need to use the terms "anti-life" or even "pro-death" for those who advocate abortion. Those who support unborn life need to be called "pro-life(ers)." Language is powerful. If we just stop to reflect for a moment before using these terms, we can cast the debate in a much more accurate light. We must start using this new language.

Anti-lifers have benefitted from this positive sounding language they have wrapped themselves in, and have made sure to use language that cast pro-lifers in a negative light. This book will use a more realistic language.

Chapter 3–The media, Hollywood, and the shaping of public opinion

Get your facts first, and then you can distort them
as much as you please. -Mark Twain

How did we get to this sad state? How was this allowed to happen? A look at the major shift in social mores and morals from the sexual revolution of the 1960's reveals the intersection of a lessening appreciation of human life and an increased emphasis on personal convenience, comfort and irresponsibility.

At one time in the United States, the goal of the press (print media and television news) was to report the news in an objective, unbiased manner. However, with the sexual revolution of the 60's, and the social shift toward liberalism, this approach appeared somewhat outdated as well as incongruous to a press eager to remake their image as more modern, liberal and exciting. The public was beginning to be offered a diet of gratuitous sex and violence at the movies and on television. The boundaries of what had been acceptable family viewing were pushed farther and farther, as networks began their liberal drift. In order to appear more cutting edge, urbane, and draw in viewers, network producers realized a shift in the media's approach was in order, which would also keep the advertising dollars flowing in. In lock step, the press also began to remake itself in a more "modern, updated, and intelligent" image as well. The message was that if you wanted to be young, smart, and popular, you embraced the new liberalism in the news, movies and television programming.

This mindset is still with us today, as we as a society have been collectively brainwashed into believing that the unexamined leftist/socialist philosophy is more intelligent and modern; as if believing it automatically raises one's I.Q. 30-40 points, and along with it, one's sense of intellectual superiority, not to mention placement in a higher social status. Peer pressure almost requires it, along with the disdain for anyone with opposing views.

There is no doubt that to a large degree, the media shapes not only public opinion, but people's social and political attitudes as well. Always eager to emulate the latest movie "stars", the public was led toward a new vision that anything "old fashioned" was to be degraded and mocked as stupid and worthless.

In his eye-opening bestseller "Hollywood vs. America," Michael Medved expertly documents how, starting in the 1960's, movies and television "stripped America of its moral compass in an all-out assault on values and sensibilities that had served the United States well for centuries." In chapters such as "A Sickness in the Soul, The Attack on Religion, The Assault on the Family, Promoting Promiscuity, Maligning Marriage, The Urge to Offend, and The Infatuation with Foul Language," Medved outlines how the depravity Hollywood foisted on us has not only desensitized us into it appearing normal, but how it has destroyed the positive foundations that have kept our society on track for centuries.

Along with graphic details of X-rated song lyrics and music videos being consumed by children as young as elementary school, Medved describes how television's glorification of indiscriminate sex with multiple random partners is depicted as a "form of recreation that has nothing to do with responsibility or commitment." This, in turn, has necessitated the quick, easy, and guilt-free "solution" of abortion, and revealed how television moguls, while fearful of a conservative backlash, are proud of this depiction:

> In 1987, Terry Louise Fisher, one of the producers of 'L.A. Law,' forthrightly expressed the attitude of the industry at large when she told *The New York Times*: 'We may be heading for a new repression, a new 'Father Knows Best' era. I hope not. For television, married or celibate characters aren't as much fun.'

> Amazingly enough, some of the industry's most respected producers take pride in such locker-room humor as a sign of the medium's new maturity. NBC executive Perry Simon argues that off-color dialogue 'is a reflection of the quality of the programs. I think it makes the audience feel it is witty and clever . . .'[10]

Medved documents how the fall lineup of television programming in 1991 reached a new low. His research illustrates how that year, the obvious message to young teens was. . .

> that all normal and healthy teenagers are sexually active well before they graduate from high school. By the end of September 1991, any American youngster who watched television with even moderate regularity would have received the unequivocal impression that the

> popular culture expected that he or she should
> become erotically experienced and cheerfully
> enter the brave new world of adolescent inter-
> course... Hollywood refuses to consider the pos-
> sibility that teenagers could be urged to avoid
> intercourse altogether ... [10]

The result is that current generations are almost unable to tell right from wrong. We are now a nation set adrift, at the mercy of the influences of violence, changed sexual attitudes, the disappearance of morals, and the cheapness of human life. This is the environment our children grow up in today, where what is left of values is uprooted, attacked, and thrown away.

For quite some time Hollywood has been teaching our children that responsibility and self-control are examples of conservative, outdated notions, and that instant gratification with no sense of responsibility or consequences is in vogue; that if you are young, modern and popular, you need neither a conscious, nor to delay gratification; that these ideas are quaint, old fashioned notions that stand in the way of "intelligent, modern" thinking. When an unexpected result of these encounters is a pregnancy, it's of no consequence, because you can just end that life if you feel it's too inconvenient.

Medved nullifies the opinion of those who have convinced themselves that children and teens are unaffected by the massmedia images they view:

> Television's portrayal of teenagers in heat typi-
> fies its power to set new standards for the society
> at large. In a nation in which the average citizen
> watches the tube for close to thirty hours each
> week, the characters on the small screen serve
> to define what constitutes normal and desirable

behavior. Children and adolescents regularly imitate heroes from television in shaping their styles of speech, dress, and grooming; it is only to be expected that they will similarly try to follow the lead of these fictional role models when it comes to intimate relationships. After many hours of programming and promos showing TV teens shedding their virginity like a shabby, childish garment they have recently outgrown, any adolescent who tried to abstain from sex would get the idea that he or she was 'weird' and hopelessly out of step.[10]

With the evolution of technology and the rise of streaming videos, podcasts, online programming, etc., Medved's figure of 30 hours of weekly television viewing is now outdated. The public may watch less television, but tunes in to media entertainment on their newest electronic device. The result is even more availability of "R" and "X" rated fare, available in laptops, smartphones, iPads, etc., that is easier to hide. Without parental controls on these devices, (and sometimes even with them), eight-year-olds with smartphones can access the most gruesome and vile horrors that can be found online.

For the many people who view these ideas as prudish, consider for a moment what "up-to-date and freedom from moralistic, repressive" thinking has brought us. According to the U.S. National Library of Medicine,

The annual number of patient consultations with private physicians in office practice for newly diagnosed symptomatic genital herpes in the USA increased 12.5-fold from 18,000 in 1966 to over 225,000 visits in 1990. From 1986 to the end of 2005, the rates of reported chlamydia infection increased from 35.2 per 100,000 to 332.5 per 100,000 population. The temporal trends have been influenced, at least in part, by changes in sexual and preventive behaviors and societal norms. [11]

Data released by the Centers for Disease Control on May 17, 1985 reveal that in 1980, there were 921,696 pregnancies among 15 to 19 year-olds, an increase of 10.5% from 1974, and for girls aged 12-14, the pregnancy rate increased 10.3% in the same period.[12]

We can hardly expect Hollywood executives to acknowledge the negative consequences for their new "morality" that earns them so many billions in box office receipts and TV advertising dollars. This breakdown of moral conscience has dramatically affected the way we and our children think about life. We have convinced ourselves that many things our society used to value are no longer important if they are too inconvenient, difficult, or require a little sacrifice. But why must an innocent pre-born child die due to his parents' irresponsibility or for their convenience?

Every year in January a huge event plays out in Washington, D.C. in the bitter cold when as many as half a million people turn out to support life and to bring to light the atrocities of abortion. The March for Life is by far the largest pro-life event in the world, and the largest annual rally our nation's capital has ever seen. From 2003 to 2009, approximately 250,000 people marched on Washington each year. In 2011, about 400,000 people participated, and in 2013, the March for Life drew an estimated 650,000 people.[13]

These numbers are staggering. However, many people have no idea such a manifestation exists, and many more are totally unaware how many individuals participate. Why? Because the press ignores the event. It's the march the mainstream liberal media doesn't want us to see. An event of this magnitude is glaringly missing from online and television news and newspapers.

It is incredible that the media refuse to devote even a few seconds to an event of this size. It's a true credit to their attempts to spin the news Americans see. As part of the anti-life media, ABC and NBC never mentioned the 2015 March for Life in its nightly news broadcast. However, a report on dogs that like to ride in motorcycle sidecars appeared in the NBC broadcast that evening. In their opinion, this was obviously more important than the more than 200,000 people rallying in Washington that day. CBS made a passing reference to it in a story on the controversy over a Republican bill on abortion.

MRC News Busters illustrates the twisted priorities and bias of our media industry: in referring to the 2014 March for Life, they state that

> the networks covered the National Zoo's baby
> panda cub six times more than that . . . In 2013,
> the networks spent 17 seconds on the March for
> Life (in comparison, they spent 521 times more
> on the Manti Te'o football scandal).[14]

When ABC, NBC, or CBS do cover the march, they ironically refuse to use the word 'life.'" The Blaze, an independent news and entertainment network with studios and offices in New York, Los Angeles, and Washington, D.C. stated that

> When it comes to the March for Life, news out-
> lets including the New York Times will generally
> keep numbers vague and low, referring to 'tens
> of thousands of protesters.' March organizers,

on the other hand, generally refer to 'hundreds
of thousands' of attendees, and some estimates
regularly top 500,000 — which would make the
March for Life one of the biggest political rallies
in American history.[15]

On February 18, 2010, an abortion facility in Philadelphia
owned and operated by Kermit Gosnell was raided by the FBI
and state police due to, among other things, suspicion of illegal
sale of prescription drugs. Inside, they found unimaginable,
horrific conditions. In his report to the Grand Jury, District
Attorney R. Seth Williams states that

When the team members entered the clinic, they
were appalled, describing it to the Grand Jury
as 'filthy, deplorable, disgusting,' very unsanitary, very outdated, horrendous,' and 'by far,
the worst' that these experienced investigators
had ever encountered. There was blood on the
floor. A stench of urine filled the air. A flea-in-
fested cat was wandering through the facility,
and there were cat feces on the stairs. Semi-
conscious women scheduled for abortions were
moaning in the waiting room or the recovery
room, where they sat on dirty recliners covered
with blood-stained blankets. All the women had
been sedated by unlicensed staff – long before
Gosnell arrived at the clinic –and staff members
could not accurately state what medications or
dosages they had administered . . . Many of the
medications in inventory were past their expi-
ration dates... surgical procedure rooms were
filthy and unsanitary... resembling 'a bad gas

station restroom.' Instruments were not sterile. Equipment was rusty and outdated ... The same corroded suction tubing used for abortions was the only tubing available for oral airways if assistance for breathing was needed...'

'[F]etal remains [were] haphazardly stored throughout the clinic– in bags, milk jugs, orange juice cartons, and even in cat-food containers... Gosnell admitted to Detective Wood that at least 10 to 20 percent... were probably older than 24 weeks [the legal limit]... In some instances, surgical incisions had been made at the base of the fetal skulls. The investigators found a row of jars containing just the severed feet of fetuses. In the basement, they discovered medical waste piled high. The intact 19-week fetus delivered by Mrs. Mongar ... was in a freezer. In all, the remains of 45 fetuses were recovered... at least two of them, and probably three, had been viable.'[16]

Gosnell performed thousands of late-term abortions, some past 30 weeks gestation. When a baby was born alive, he severed the spinal cord. Ultimately, he was charged with seven counts of first-degree murder, including a woman to whom a lethal dose of anesthesia had been administered, and one count of third-degree murder, among several other charges. He had a string of prior complaints and citations dating back to 1989. He had been censured and fined for employing unlicensed personnel and patient death due to negligence, among other atrocities. He had 46 known lawsuits filed against him over the course of 32 years. There were many cases of near-death of patients. Just one example was a late-term abortion performed on a woman whose pain was so unbearable four days later, that she could barely walk. Ultrasound showed pieces of the fetus still left inside her uterus, which Gosnell suctioned out without anesthesia.

This horrific example is not given here to imply that this is typical of all abortion clinics; it is not. It is cited as another example of the pro-abortion press intentionally hiding the seediest aspects of abortion from the public, especially second and third trimester abortions. In the April 11, 2013 edition of USA Today, Kristen Powers wrote

> A Lexis-Nexis search shows none of the news shows on the three major national television networks has mentioned the Gosnell trial in the last three months, and that national press coverage was represented by a *Wall Street Journal* columnist who 'hijacked' a segment on *Meet the Press*, a single page A-17 story on the first day of the trial by *The New York Times*, and no original coverage by *The Washington Post.*[17]

It was only after a Twitter campaign launched by pro-life advocates showing rows of empty media seats in the courtroom did mainstream media grudgingly and briefly include it in their coverage.

Intentional media blackout of pro-life issues is another reason why almost no one in the United States ever knew that Congresswoman Marsha Blackburn and 71 other members of Congress signed a letter in April, 2013 condemning the media bias in choosing to ignore the Gosnell case.[18]

Another detail conveniently absent from media coverage was uncovered on May 17, 2015 by the Huffington Post:

The grand jury report said that one look at the place would have detected the problems, but the Pennsylvania Department of Health hadn't inspected the place since 1993. Here's the grand jury report . . .

The Pennsylvania Department of Health abruptly decided, for political reasons, to stop inspecting abortion clinics at all. The politics in question were not anti-abortion, but pro. With the change of administration from Governor Casey to (pro-abortion) Governor Ridge, officials concluded that inspections would be 'putting a barrier up to women' seeking abortions.

'Even nail salons in Pennsylvania are monitored more closely for client safety,' the report states. 'Without regular inspections, providers like Gosnell continue to operate; unlawful and dangerous third-trimester abortions go undetected; and many women, especially poor women, suffer'.[19]

Pro-abortion media obviously aren't the only ones trying to hide the horrors of abortion. Their anti-life political allies have as much, or more blood on their hands as well. In their groundbreaking book "The Media Elite – America's New Powerbrokers," Robert Lichter, a research professor in political science at George Washington University, Linda Lichter, co-director of the Center for Media and Public Affairs in Washington, D.C., and Stanley Rothman, the Mary Huggins Gamble Professor of Government at Smith College, conducted an exhaustive and landmark analysis of the media elites who control the manner in which the public receives national and international news. Their book, "the first systemic study of the people who tell us most of what we know about the world around us" is a fascinating examination of hundreds of leading journalists from the New York Times, the Wall Street Journal, the Washington Post, Time, Newsweek, U.S. News and World Report, and the news departments at ABC, CBS, NBC and PBS.

Their lengthy empirical study had two main objectives: "a survey of the backgrounds, attitudes, and psychological traits of journalists at national media outlets, and content analysis of how these outlets covered some of the major social controversies of the past fifteen years."[20]

They document how the press and media in the United States evolved in the twentieth century, and how the emergence of the media elite's "expanded role, and the social changes underlying it, are responsible for the new elite status that the national media now enjoy." They accomplished this task by combining "the approaches of social theory and social science, the methods of survey research and content analysis and the perspectives of political sociology and social psychology."

They describe how nowhere was this evolution of media elites more dramatic than on television. As the age of television began, it was "dominated immediately by the three major networks centered in New York. Given the expense of producing programs, local stations came to depend on the networks for both entertainment and news programs."[20]

The networks were successful, as the Lichters and Rothman described, with "the bottom line . . . capturing audience attention and increasing the size of audiences. This is what produces profits and ensures solvency."

The explosion in television ownership in the 1950's and 60's undoubtedly brought one of the most profound social shifts in the history of the United States. It was then, Lichter states, that

> the United States was beginning to develop a national media network; that is, a relatively small group of media outlets was increasingly determining the manner in which the world was being presented to Americans. And these outlets were largely centered in New York and, for political news, Washington.[20]

The stage was therefore set for an enormous social change in the United States. Since media control was centered in a few major urban areas of the country, Lichter explains that

> ... the influence of new metropolitan styles created in New York and Los Angeles, spread(s) far more rapidly than it once did ... Insofar as those who live on New York's upper East Side or in Los Angeles help create the reality America sees, so they help change the expectations and outlooks of Americans. . . . The combination of unprecedented affluence and intellectual and cultural sophistication produced a cosmopolitan sensibility that clashed sharply with the verities of small-town America.[20]

The values of heartland and mainstream America were derided as boring, outdated, conservative and intellectually inferior. Wikipedia has described in detail, the "rural purge" of television programs in the late 1960s and early 70s. The "young, urban demographic" was seen as the new desired consumer of television airtime. Programs such as Lassie, The Andy Griffith

Show, My Three Sons, The Wild Kingdom, Petticoat Junction, The Beverly Hillbillies, and Green Acres were only a few of the still popular, highly rated shows that were cancelled. Some of the shows that replaced the cancelled ones "were never truly ratings hits" but "appealed to a younger demographic and thus were renewed" for additional seasons. The Licters and Rothman describe how

> This narrowing cultural gap has played an important role in weakening traditional ties of church, ethnic group and neighborhood. . . It is impossible to understand the revolution that took place in American values and attitudes during the 1960s and 1970s without taking into account the influence of television on the fabric of American life. For the first time metropolitan America was becoming all of America.[20]

Media experts Thomas Patterson and Ronald Abeles were concerned that "decisions about what the public will know rest increasingly upon the beliefs of the small elite which determines what they should know."[21]

In his book "Making Something of Ourselves", Richard Merelman went a step further in describing how the liberal east coast media elites shaped public opinion in their image: "Americans' primordial ties to family, locality, church and what is considered appropriate behavior have eroded, and Americans have lost their sense of place."

Instead of simply reporting the facts or events in the United States, Lichter explains that "Good reporting seemed to permit or even require a point of view and a choice of one side against the other." Of course, the media elite made careful efforts to take a stand on current and controversial issues that appeared urbane, progressive, liberal and correct. Lichter says that

> In the years that followed Watergate, the national media rode a wave of popularity and perceived power. They appeared to have chosen the 'right' side in the critical conflicts of a turbulent decade. .. They were courted by politicians and revered on college campuses.

So who are these media elite and what do they believe? Ninety percent believed that

> a woman has (the) right to decide on abortion. .. A distinctive characteristic of the Media Elite is its secular outlook . . . Very few are regular churchgoers. Only 8 percent go to church or syn-agogue weekly, and 86 percent seldom or never attend religious services... substantial numbers of the media elite grew up at a distance from the social and cultural traditions of small-town middle America. Instead, they came from big cities in the northeast and north central states. Their parents were mostly well off, highly edu-cated members of the upper middle class, espe-cially the educated professions. In short, they are a highly cosmopolitan group, with differentially eastern, urban, ethnic, upper-status, and sec-ular roots.[20]

These findings led Lichter to feel that the media elite "are united in rejecting social conservatism and traditional norms and their support for social liberalism", and that "the media elite's perspective is predominantly cosmopolitan and liberal," even though Lichter's research was conducted at a time when "conservatives outnumbered liberals by 31 to 17 percent" in the general American public.

Other surveys also report the disparity between the social/ political makeup of the press versus the wider public. A study conducted at California State University, Los Angeles in 1982 on journalists at America's fifty largest newspapers already found self-described liberals far outweighing conservatives.[22]

When relying on sources for their news reporting, Lichter found that the media elites' "choices were weighted heavily toward the liberal end. Three out of four journalists mention at least one liberal source. In sharp contrast, fewer than one in four cites a conservative source."

Their empirical research points out that "a surprising number of leading journalists are willing to admit to problems of bias, at least in principle." A "slight majority" even believe that they themselves should play "a major role" in promoting social reform.

This narcissism is illustrated in one of the surveys Lichter conducted, which asked journalists to rank the amount of influence various groups should have over the direction society should take. The media elites ranked themselves "as the group most favored to influence American society. . . . A majority of the journalists surveyed believe their work should be a force for social reform." Columnist Joseph Kraft agrees. . .

> We (the media elite) are highly prone to that disease of the times – narcissism. The narcissism of the journalist, of course, is not mere conceit. It consists in the belief that because we describe events, we make them happen.[23]

In his work "The Imperial Media" Kraft also observes

> We no longer represent a wide diversity of views.
> We have ceased to be neutral in reporting events
> . . . . increases in the social, economic, and educa-
> tional status of journalists are linked to liberal or
> anti-establishment attitudes.[23]

Still another prominent columnist of the time, Henry Fairlie, describes just how powerful the Washington D.C. media elites have become:

> The most certain avenue to celebrity and con-
> siderable wealth (in Washington) is not now in
> the institution of government . . . It is through
> the intricate networks of the media . . . the
> people of the media are today the wheelers and
> dealers. Point to any others so skillful at using
> the machinery of Washington, and so protected
> from any public challenge or scrutiny . . . The
> media have removed themselves from all contact
> in their daily lives with the ordinary middle-class
> life and tastes of the community.[24]

Daniel Moynihan, PhD, Democratic senator, Harvard professor, and U.S. ambassador to the United Nations, corroborated with this observation:

> Journalism has become, if not an elite profes-
> sion, a profession attractive to elites. This is
> noticeably so in Washington, where the upper
> reaches of journalism constitute one of the most
> important and enduring social elites of the city,

with all the accoutrements one associates with
the leisured class . . . . the political consequences
of the rising social status of journalism is that the
press grows more and more influenced by attitudes genuinely hostile to society and American
government.[25]

It comes as no surprise that this egocentrism might result
in the media elites feeling they have free reign to present what
happens in the world through their own filter. As Lichter puts
it, "Another alleged result of wealth and celebrity is a sense of
self-importance that redefines the role of journalists as news-
makers themselves," and illustrates this point with an incidence
from the 1984 presidential campaign: Dan Rather was inter-
viewing Alan Cranston, senator and presidential candidate,
when a CBS aide informed Mr. Cranston that " . . . Mr. Rather
will only have time for one more question."

Lichter continues, "In keeping with their newfound status,
leading journalists are increasingly likely to see themselves as
professionals who translate the news rather than craftsmen
who merely transmit it." In fact, the Lichters found that in each
instance of the media's coverage of three social issues: nuclear
power, busing, and the oil industry's role in the energy crisis,
"the coverage diverged from the expert assessments in the
direction of the media elite's own perspectives . . . . In every
instance the coverage followed neither the middle path nor the
expert evidence."

It should be pointed out that the Lichters' and Rothman's
research was conducted in the mid-1980's. However, instead of
discounting it as outdated, consider the fact that it was written
shortly after these enormous social changes were happening.
As societal values have undoubtedly continued to shift, the
observation can be made that the change in composition of

the media elite has continued its trend that started 55 years ago, becoming even more extreme in their political beliefs and egocentrism. The Lichters and Rothman themselves believed "These characteristics will likely become more pronounced in the future."

This prediction is illustrated by the results of another survey the Lichters and Rothman conducted on the backgrounds and attitudes of journalism students enrolled at Columbia University in New York City at the time of their research. Among that group, who would be today's journalists, 82% were from metropolitan areas, 85% self-identified as liberal, 11% conservative, and 46% had no religion. Seventy-five percent believed that the "U.S. exploits (the) Third World, (and) causes poverty" and 96% believe that a "woman has (the) right to decide on abortion." Lichter's research found that these students "rate Cuban Premier Fidel Castro almost as highly as (Margaret) Thatcher, and considerably more positively than Ronald Regan."

Media persecution of conservative and pro-life organizations has only become more widespread in recent years. Brad Parscale, a digital consultant and political aide, wrote the following in an opinion column for USA Today:

> Americans must be wary of powerful institutions that seek to control what we see and hear. As the internet has become an increasingly central part of modern life, Big Tech giants such as Facebook, Twitter and Google have increasingly sought to become the gatekeepers of the internet and political discourse.
>
> Without any sort of democratic mandate, these companies have appointed themselves the arbiters of acceptable thought, discussion and

searches online. These companies' pervasive command of the internet — and blatant desire to control how we interact with it, is a direct threat to a free society. And arguably the worst offender is Google.

Google claims to value free expression and a free and open internet, but there is overwhelming evidence that the Big Tech giant wants the internet to be free and open only to political and social ideas of which it approves.

Google & others are suppressing voices of conservatives and hiding information and news that is good. They are controlling what we can and cannot see.

Also, research at Harvard University found that Google's search rankings are not objective, and in 2017, the company was fined billions of dollars by the European Union for manipulating search results.

Google also maintains at least nine shadowy blacklists that affect what the public sees when using its search engine.

When it's not manipulating the internet to prevent users from viewing right-wing content, Google is directly attacking that content. A report by The Daily Caller News Foundation revealed that Google's fact-checking service "fact-checked" only conservative news websites, and that in many cases, these fact-checks were outright wrong. What does it say about the fact-checker when its fact-checking is biased and incorrect?

Sometimes, the tech giant just attacks conservatives directly. In one infamous example, a Google search result listed "Nazism" as an official ideology of the California GOP. North Carolina Sen. Trudy Wade, a Republican, was shocked to discover that the top search result for her name returned a photo labeling her as a bigot.

If something vaguely conservative and intellectually stimulating manages to get past Google's content gatekeepers, they just remove it. YouTube, which is owned by Google, routinely demonizes, restricts and censors conservative content. One target of YouTube was Dennis Prager's PragerU, which had 40 of its videos restricted. Prager sued the social media video giant this year following these unfounded restrictions. YouTube has also been known for banning pro-life videos.

Google's eager adoption of the role of censor should come as little surprise. Eric Schmidt, the executive chairman of Google's parent company, Alphabet Inc., has a demonstrated track record of combining the role of Democrat activist with his job.

Wikileaks emails revealed that Schmidt worked directly with the Clinton campaign in 2016 and was instrumental in forming "The Groundwork," an online startup company created to help Clinton win the election. He was also seen wearing a 'staff badge' at the Clinton election night party.

While President Barack Obama was in office, Google kept a cozy relationship with the White House. Google representatives attended White House meetings more than once a week during the first seven years of Obama's presidency, and almost 250 individuals left government service to work for Google or vice versa while Obama was in office. The Obama administration may also have squashed an antitrust investigation into the company.

Google's nefarious activities should concern not just conservatives and Republicans, but every American who values free speech and a truly free and open internet.

Google's broad and pervasive role in the lives of almost every American today cannot be overstated. More than 90 percent of all online searches are conducted through Google or YouTube. The media giant's video-sharing site has 1 billion active users per month, many of whom go there to learn and share conservative ideas only to find their quest for knowledge sub-verted by faceless ideologues.

Google is clearly manipulating and controlling the political narrative in favor of Democrats and the left, and silencing conservatives and Republicans. A company with such power and influence cannot simply be allowed to play the biased gatekeeper of political discourse.[26]

In an article for LifeNews.com, Ashley Rae Goldenberg and Dan Gainor reveal that

> Like it or not, social media is the communication form of the future–not just in the U.S., but world-wide. Just Facebook and Twitter combined reach 1.8 billion people. More than two-thirds of all Americans (68 percent) use Facebook. YouTube is pushing out TV as the most popular place to watch video. Google is the No. 1 search engine in both the U.S. and the world.

> War is being declared on the conservative move-ment in this space and conservatives are losing–badly. If the right is silenced, billions of people will be cut off from conservative ideas and con-servative media.

> It's the new battleground of media bias. But it's worse. That bias is not a war of ideas. It's a war against ideas. It's a clear effort to censor the conservative worldview from the public conversation.

> The Media Research Center has undertaken an extensive study of the problem at major tech companies–Twitter, Facebook, Google and YouTube–and the results are far more troubling

than most conservatives realize. Here are some of the key findings:

Twitter Leads in Censorship: Project Veritas recently had caught Twitter staffers admitting on hidden camera that they had been censoring conservatives through a technique known as shadow banning, where users think their content is getting seen widely, but it's not. The staffers had justified it by claiming the accounts had been automated if they had words such as 'America' and 'God.' In 2016, Twitter had attempted to manipulate election-related tweets using the hashtags "#PodestaEmails" and "#DNCLeak." The site also restricts pro-life ads from Live Action and even Rep. Marsha Blackburn (R-Tenn.), but allows Planned Parenthood advertisements.

Facebook's Trending Feed Has Been Hiding Conservative Topics: A 2016 Gizmodo story had warned of Facebook's bias. It had detailed claims by former employees that Facebook's news curators had been instructed to hide conservative content from the 'trending' section, which supposedly only features news users find compelling. Topics that had been blacklisted included Mitt Romney, the Conservative Political Action Conference (CPAC) and Rand Paul. On the other hand, the term 'Black Lives Matter' had also been placed into the trending section even though it was not actually trending. Facebook had also banned at least one far right European organization but had not released information on any specific statements made by the group that warranted the ban.

Google Search Aids Democrats: Google and YouTube's corporate chairman Eric Schmidt had assisted Hillary Clinton's presidential campaign. The company's search engine had deployed a similar bias in favor of Democrats. One study had found 2016 campaign searches were biased in favor of Hillary Clinton. Even the liberal website Slate had revealed the search engine's results had favored both Clinton and Democratic candidates. Google also had fired engineer James Damore for criticizing the company's 'Ideological Echo Chamber.' The company had claimed he had been fired for 'advancing harmful gender stereotypes in our workplace.' Damore is suing Google, saying it mistreats whites, males and conservatives.

YouTube Is Shutting Down Conservative Videos: Google's YouTube site had created its own problems with conservative content. YouTube moderators must take their cues from the rest of Google – from shutting down entire conservative channels 'by mistake' to removing videos that promote right-wing political views. YouTube's special Creators for Change section is devoted to people using their 'voices for social change' and even highlights the work of a 9/11 truther.

Tech Firms Are Relying on Groups That Hate Conservatives: Top tech firms like Google, YouTube and Twitter partner with leftist groups attempting to censor conservatives. These include the Southern Poverty Law Center (SPLC) and the Anti-Defamation League (ADL). Both groups claim to combat 'hate,' but treat standard conservative beliefs in faith and family as examples of that hatred. George Soros-funded ProPublica is using information from both radical leftist organizations to attack conservative groups such as Jihad Watch and ACT for America, bullying PayPal and other services to shut down their funding sources. The SPLC's 'anti-LGBT' list had also been used to prevent organizations from partnering with AmazonSmile to raise funds.

Liberal Twitter Advisors Outnumber Conservatives 12-to-1: Twelve of the 25 U.S. members of Twitter's Trust and Safety Council – which helps guide its policies – are liberal, and only one is conservative. Anti-conservative groups like GLAAD and the ADL are part of the board. There is no well-known conservative group represented.

Tech Companies Rely on Anti-Conservative Fact-Checkers: Facebook and Google both had partnered with fact-checking organizations in order to combat 'fake news.' Facebook's short-lived disputed flagger program had allowed Snopes, PolitiFact and ABC News to discern what is and is not real news. Google's fact-checkers had accused conservative sources of making claims that did not appear in their articles and disproportionately 'fact-checked' conservative sources. On Facebook, a satire site, the Babylon Bee, had been flagged by Snopes for its article clearly mocking CNN for its bias. YouTube also had announced a partner- ship with Wikipedia in order to debunk videos deemed to be conspiracy theories, even though Wikipedia has been criticized for its liberal bias.[26]

By the beginning of 2020, it had become blatantly obvious that a great majority of mainstream media in the United States no longer reported the news in an unbiased manner, but has turned into a propaganda arm of the political left. They have continuous hatred of anything and anyone conservative, especially President Trump. Air time that used to be devoted to reporting on newsworthy apolitical stories now offer a constant stream of extremist liberal ranting, often with no effort at verifying the veracity of their claims. Even brief, grudging reporting on politically conservative successes is completely absent. While the spin on the news described by the Lichters and Rothman used to be subtle, the biased attacks on the President and the Republican party are now brazen, transparent, and obvious. No attempt is even made to disguise them as anything else. This is what passes for "news" at the beginning of the second decade of the 21st century.

Chapter 4–Types of abortion and legal implications

And although no one remembers exactly how it happened, the unthinkable becomes tolerable. And then acceptable. And then legal. And then applaudable. – Joni Eareckson Tada

For over four decades, Planned Parenthood and other abortionists have been extremely successful at lying to the public about what really happens during an abortion. This deliberate cover up has served them well. We have been lulled into an innocently ignorant state of believing that an abortion is a "gentle suctioning of the contents of the uterus" as Planned Parenthood claims.

Believing for so long Planned Parenthood's sanitized version of what happens in an abortion had successfully neutered any large-scale opposition from the public until the mid-2010's. More than 40 largely unopposed years of abortion on demand has led to its entrenchment in our society that is almost impossible to eradicate.

We cannot have a discussion of abortion or any other topic without having a clear idea of what it is we're talking about. We cannot change hearts and minds unless we have the facts surrounding what abortion really is.

Many pro-lifers become queasy and recoil when confronted visually with the gore and violence of abortion. "Oh, I can't look at that" is a common response. Let's be clear: An issue cannot be effectively defended or discredited unless we know what it is that we're trying to defend or discredit. To know in the abstract is a beginning. To experience it by seeing it gives us access to the reality of, in this case, abortion. If everyone could witness an abortion, either in person, or with photographs or videos, this book would not have to be written.

Almost no pro-death proponents, or pro-lifers for that matter, have seen the grisly aftermath of an abortion: the bloody, dismembered, decapitated, completely formed baby. These images and videos are readily available with a quick online search. Overlay the shock and horror of seeing aborted babies with the even more shocking fact that this is not the result of an accident. More than one person purposely chose the results seen in these pictures and videos.

This aversion and the imposed ignorance on the public by abortionists, has only served to hide the realities of abortion. It has only served the purposes of Planned Parenthood and weakened the pro-life resolve. As long as we refuse to acknowledge what happens in an abortion, as long as we choose not to stand up against it, as long as civic and religious leaders refuse to talk about it, teach about it, and pretend it doesn't exist, abortion will always be with us.

To lay some basic groundwork, let us pull back the curtain and examine what actually happens during an abortion. There are several different abortion procedures, and the one the abortionist uses is usually determined by how far a woman's pregnancy has advanced.

Dr. Anthony Levatino is a board-certified obstetrician-gynecologist with 40 years of medical experience. He performed 1,200 abortions before having a pro-life conversion. He is now one of the most quoted experts in pro-life circles. His following descriptions of first, second, and third trimester abortions come from his vast store of medical knowledge and experience. The following are transcriptions of one of his Youtube videos.

First trimester medical abortion. This is a procedure in which the mother swallows pills in order to terminate her baby and it is performed up to the ninth week of pregnancy. The procedure involves two steps.

Step one: at the abortion clinic or doctor's office, the woman takes pills which contain Mifepristone, also called RU46. RU46 blocks the action of a hormone called progesterone. Progesterone is naturally produced in the mother's body to stabilize the lining of the uterus. When RU46 blocks progesterone, the lining of the mother's uterus breaks down, cutting off blood and nourishment to the baby who then dies inside the mother's womb. It is important to note, that even after it has been taken, it is possible to reverse the effects of RU46 and save the baby if progesterone is administered, the sooner the better.

Step two: 24-48 hours after taking RU46, the woman takes misoprostol, also called cytotec, that is administered either orally or vaginally. RU46 and misoprostol together cause severe cramping, contractions, and often heavy bleeding, to force the dead baby out of the woman's uterus. The process can be very intense and painful, and the bleeding and contractions could last from a few hours to several days. While she could lose her baby at anytime and anywhere during this process, the woman will often sit on a toilet as she prepares to expel the child, which she will then flush. She may even see her dead baby within the pregnancy sac. At nine weeks for example, the baby will be almost an inch long, and if she looks carefully, she might be able to count the fingers and toes. After she has disposed of her baby, the woman may have bleeding and spotting for several weeks. Bleeding lasts on average, nine to 16 days. Eight percent of women bleed more than 30 days, and one percent require hospitalization because of heavy bleeding.

RU46 is only FDA approved for the first seven weeks of pregnancy. While RU46 can be used off label up to nine weeks, the failure rate increases as the pregnancy progresses. At seven weeks, it has a five percent failure rate, at eight weeks an eight percent failure rate, and at nine weeks a 10 percent failure rate. If failure occurs, she will usually be offered a surgical abortion. For the mother, medical abortion often causes abdominal pain, nausea, vomiting, diarrhea, headache, and heavy bleeding. Maternal deaths have occurred, most frequently due to infection and undiagnosed ectopic pregnancy.

<u>First trimester surgical abortion</u> called suction D and C, dilation and curettage. This is the most frequently performed abortion and is used typically from five to thirteen weeks of pregnancy.

After administering anesthesia, the abortionist uses a speculum, like this. This is placed inside the vagina and opened using this screw on the side, allowing the abortionist to see the cervix, the entrance to the uterus. The cervix acts as a gate, that stays closed for the duration of pregnancy, protecting the baby until it is ready for birth. The abortionist uses a series of metal rods called dilators like these, which increase in thickness and inserts them into the cervix to dilate it, gaining access to the inside of the uterus, where the baby resides. The baby has a heartbeat, fingers, toes, arms and legs, but it's bones are still weak and fragile. The abortionist takes a suction catheter, like this one. This is a 14 french suction catheter. It's clear plastic, about nine inches long and it has a hole through the center. It is inserted through the cervix into the uterus. The suction machine is then turned on with a force 10 to 20 times more powerful than your household vacuum cleaner. The baby is rapidly torn apart by the force of the suction and squeezed through this tubing down into the suction machine, followed by the placenta. Though the uterus is mostly emptied at this point, one of the risks of a suction D and C is incomplete abortion, essentially pieces of the baby or placenta left behind. This can lead to infection or bleeding. In an attempt to prevent this, the abortionist uses a curette to scrape the lining of the uterus. The curette is basically a long handled curved blade. Once the uterus is empty, the speculum is removed and the abortion is complete.

The risks of suction D and C include perforation or laceration of the uterus or cervix, potentially damaging the intestine, bladder and nearby blood vessels, hemorrhage, infection, and in rare instances, even death. Future pregnancies are also at a greater risk for loss or premature delivery due to abortion related trauma and injury to the cervix.[27]

Anti-life websites such as *emedicinehealth* and Planned Parenthood always offer a "sanitized" description of abortion, glossing over the gruesome details, so as to make it more palatable to the general public. They call early abortions "menstrual extractions", likening it to a menstrual period, sounding very benign, when in actuality, it is still an abortion. They refer to the embryo/fetus as "products of conception", "contents of the uterus", or "tissue". In reality, in the first six weeks after conception, this "tissue" has formed internal organs including a beating heart, lungs, brain, blood cells, nerve cells and spinal cord.[28] The callousness with which these anti-life websites describe an abortion is chilling. *Emedicinehealth* claims that

Women who select a medical abortion express a slightly greater satisfaction with their route of abortion and, in the majority of cases, express a wish to choose this method again should they have another abortion.[29]

Dr. Levatino goes on to describe how second trimester abortions are performed.

Second trimester surgical abortion called dilatation and evacuation (D&E). A D&E is performed from between 13 and 24 weeks of pregnancy. After administering anesthesia, the abortionist uses a weighted speculum . . . that opens the vagina widely. Because second trimester babies are so large, this greater access facilitates a late term abortion. Late term abortion requires that the cervix be prepared 24 to 48 hours in advance with laminaria. Laminaria is a type of sterilized seaweed that absorbs water over 8 to 12 hours and swells to several times its original diameter. Once removed, metal dilators can be used to further open the cervix as needed. Once the cervix has been stretched open, the suction tube is placed inside. A baby at 20 weeks gestation is as big as the length of my hand, from head to rump, not counting the legs. The suction machine is turned on, and pale yellow amniotic fluid surrounding the baby is suctioned out through the catheter. But babies this big, they don't fit through catheters this size. The baby's bones and skull are too strong to be torn apart by suction alone.[27]

At this point in the video, Dr. Levatino shows us a simple but gruesome instrument called a sopher clamp. It was invented in England by a Dr. Sopher with the sole purpose of obtaining a better grasp on baby body parts. Dr. Levatino describes it as being

. . . made of stainless steel, it's about 13 inches long. The business end is about two and a half inches long and a half inch wide and there are rows of sharp teeth. This is a grasping instrument; when it gets ahold of something, it does not let go. The abortionist uses this clamp to grasp an arm or a leg. Once he has a firm grip, the abortionist pulls hard, in order to tear the limb from the baby's body. One by one, the rest of the limbs are removed, along with the intestines, the spine, and the heart and lungs. Usually the most difficult part of the procedure is extracting the baby's head, which is about the size of a large plum at 20 weeks. The head is grasped and crushed. The abortionist knows he has crushed the skull when a white substance comes out of the cervix. This was the baby's brains. The abortionist then removes skull pieces. He removes the placenta and any leftover parts of the baby with a curette, scraping the lining of the uterus for any remaining tissue. The abortionist then collects the baby parts and reassembles them, to make sure that there are two arms, two legs, and all the pieces. Once all the parts have been accounted for, the abortion is complete.

For the woman, this procedure carries a significant risk of major complications, including perforation or laceration of the uterus or cervix, with possible damage to the bowel, bladder, and other maternal organs. Infection and hemorrhage can also occur, which can even lead to death. Future pregnancies are also at greater risk for loss or premature delivery, due to abortion related trauma and injury to the cervix.[27]

This happens on a fetus that by 13-24 weeks, has hair forming on his head, a liver and pancreas that are already producing secretions, is beginning to move and stretch, and is making sucking noises, according to MedlinePlus Medical Encyclopedia.[28] At this point, the medical research is inconclusive as to when a fetus can detect pain, but many experts have gone on record as saying that the unborn are capable of feeling pain as early as 20 weeks gestation.

Finally, Dr. Levatino describes a third trimester induced abortion, which occurs at 25 weeks to delivery:

> At this point, the baby is almost fully developed and viable, meaning he or she could survive outside the womb if the mother were to go into labor prematurely. Because the baby is so large and developed, this procedure takes 3 or 4 days to complete. On day one the abortionist uses a large needle to inject a drug called Digoxin. Digoxin is generally used to treat heart problems, but a high enough dosage of Digoxin will cause fatal cardiac arrest. The abortionist inserts the needle with the Digoxin through the woman's abdomen or through her vagina and into the baby, targeting either the head, torso or heart. The baby will feel it. Babies at this stage feel pain. When the needle pierces the baby's body and the Digoxin takes effect, the life of the baby will end. The abortionist then inserts multiple sticks of seaweed called laminaria into the woman's cervix. They will slowly open up the cervix for the delivery of a stillborn baby. While the woman waits for the laminaria to dilate her cervix, she carries her dead baby inside of her for two to three days.

On day two, the abortionist replaces the laminaria and may perform a second ultrasound to ensure the baby is dead. If the child is still alive, he administers another lethal dose of Digoxin. The woman then goes back to where she is staying while her cervix continues to dilate. If she goes into labor and is unable to make it to the clinic in time, she will give birth at home or in a hotel. In this case, she may be advised to deliver her baby into a bathroom toilet. The abortionist then comes to remove the baby and clean up. If she can make it to the clinic, she will do so during her most severe contractions, and deliver her dead son or daughter. If the baby does not come out whole, then the procedure becomes a D & E, a dilation and evacuation, and the abortionist uses clamps and forceps to dismember the baby, piece by piece. Once the placenta and all the body parts have been removed, the abortion is complete.

Late term abortions have a high risk of hemorrhage, lacerations, and uterine perforations, as well as a risk of maternal death. Future pregnancies are also at a greater risk for loss or premature delivery due to abortion related trauma and injury to the cervix.[27]

One of the most abhorrent and heinous type of abortion, however, whose details pro-death proponents have long tried to keep from the public, is the late term procedure called "dilation and extraction" (D & X) or "partial birth abortion". Emedicine health describes this procedure as involving cervical dilation, after which the "fetus is removed in a mostly intact condition. The fetal head is able to be collapsed after the contents are evacuated so that it may pass through the cervix."[29] Again, the sanitized version leaves out the details that are far too graphic for even some anti-life proponents, as described below.

The legalities of partial birth abortion are complicated. The confusion and complexity arise from the precise verbiage used in bills presented for vote by Congress. Most of the discrepancies in different versions of these bills have to do with exceptions for the health of the mother. Many liberal politicians in the past have not voted to ban the procedure due to lack of exceptions for the physical health of the mother, although medical research and practitioners have shown that late term abortions past the point of fetal viability outside the womb are never necessary. The doctor simply induces labor and delivers a live baby. Confusion also arose over the use of the word "health", some claiming that it needed more precise definition. Anti-life proponents argued that the "health" exemption needed to include mental health. It was this exemption, along with its vagueness, that soon began facilitating partial birth abortions in situations where the term "mental health" had a very broad and loose interpretation, such as the mother feeling that giving birth to a live baby would cause her depression. Most abortion laws are further complicated by the fact that individual states can and do pass their own legislation, either restricting or expanding abortion within their borders.

In any case, public opposition to partial birth abortions grew during the 1990s until Florida Representative Charles T. Canady introduced a bill to ban it in 1995. Both houses of Congress approved versions of the bill in 1996 and 1997. However, President Clinton vetoed both bans. The House overrode Clinton's veto, but the Senate was several votes short in opposing it. The Partial-Birth Abortion Ban act was finally passed by Congress in 2003, and signed into law by President George W. Bush. Its constitutionality was upheld by the Supreme Court case of Gonzales v. Carhart in 2007. To substantiate their ruling, the Court quoted an eyewitness account, which is in stark contrast to the above description by Emedicine health:

> Dr. Haskell went in with forceps and grabbed the baby's legs and pulled them down into the birth canal. Then he delivered the baby's body and the arms – everything but the head. The doctor kept the head right inside the uterus. . . . The baby's little fingers were clasping and unclasping, and his little feet were kicking. Then the doctor struck the scissors in the back of his head, and the baby's arms jerked out, like a startle reaction, like a flinch, like a baby does when he thinks he is going to fall. The doctor opened up the scissors, stuck a high-powered suction tube into the opening, and sucked the baby's brains out. Now the baby went completely limp. . . . He cut the umbilical cord and delivered the placenta. He threw the baby in a pan, along with the placenta and the instruments he had just used.[30]

Congress called it a "gruesome and inhumane procedure that is never medically necessary and should be prohibited." Additionally, the Legal Information Institute at Cornell University states that after exhaustive research from medical professionals including former Surgeon General C. Everett Koop, Congress' conclusions were that partial-birth abortions

> are not only unnecessary to preserve the health of the mother, but in fact, poses serious risks to

the long-term health of women and in some circumstances, their lives . . . the facts indicate that
a partial-birth abortion is never necessary to
preserve the health of a woman, poses serious
risks to a woman's health, and lies outside the
standard of medical care, and should, therefore,
be banned.[31]

Anti-life forces were furious, mounting an immediate legal
appeal, claiming that the procedure was almost never performed, and then only to save the life of the mother. Again,
this was not true. Planned Parenthood's own research and
policy division, the Guttmacher Institute, revealed that there
were 2,200 partial-birth abortions performed in 2000.[32] The
Guttmacher Institute was called out on even these figures in
1997 by Ron Fitzsimmons, executive director of the National
Coalition of Abortion Providers, stating that approximately
5,000 partial-birth abortions were performed annually, with
"the vast majority of these abortions entirely elective, performed on healthy mothers and destroying healthy babies in
the fifth or sixth month of gestation."[33]

To circumvent the restrictions on partial birth abortions,
abortionists created other means to end a late term pregnancy,
as with the Digoxin injections to kill the baby, described by Dr.
Levatino. Emedicinehealth described another alternative to
this gruesome and barbaric procedure that gets around local
legal limitations:

To avoid performing a partial birth abortion
while performing a legal dilation and extraction,
digitalis or potassium chloride may be injected
into the fetus to induce preoperative fetal death.
Fetal cord cutting may accomplish this as well.[29]

We are left to assume that emedicinehealth feels this is a better way to squirm around the law and kill a viable unborn baby that can feel pain. They, along with many in the pro-death groups, have defended partial birth abortions of late-term babies since the carnage began, making arguments so absurd in its defense, we can only wonder at their sanity. They blindly cling to the delusion that abortion on demand, including partial-birth abortion, is a freedom every woman should enjoy, ignoring all the truths. As Ben Shapiro observed, if you kill a newborn baby, you go to jail for murder. If you abort the same baby in utero 24 hours earlier, anti-lifers call it a human right.

The following observations are taken from a section on late-term abortion from research presented in the Journal of American Medical Association.

> ...ethical concerns have been raised about intact
> D&X. The viability of the fetus and the time
> when viability is achieved may vary with each
> pregnancy. In the second trimester when via-
> bility may be in question, it is the physician who
> should determine the viability of a specific fetus,
> using the latest available diagnostic technology.
> In recognition of the constitutional principles
> regarding the right to an abortion articulated by
> the Supreme Court in <u>Roe v. Wade</u>, and in keeping
> with the science and values of medicine, the AMA
> recommends that abortions not be performed
> in the third trimester except in cases of serious
> fetal anomalies incompatible with life. Although
> third-trimester abortions can be performed to
> preserve the life or health of the mother, they are,
> in fact, generally not necessary for those pur-
> poses. Except in extraordinary circumstances,

maternal health factors which demand termination of the pregnancy can be accommodated without sacrifice of the fetus, and the near certainty of the independent viability of the fetus argues for ending the pregnancy by appropriate delivery.[34]

However, liberal courts chose to ignore expert medical testimony that partial-birth abortion is not necessary to preserve the health of a woman, and the 2003 ban began to fail several legal challenges due to the lack of such a "health exception". This is in spite of a Gallup poll from January, 2003 that found that 70% of the public favored a ban on partial-birth abortions.[35] Descriptions of abortions from nurse eyewitnesses intimately involved in the procedure are numerous and stand in enormous contrast to the glossed-over and sanitized versions we get from pro-death providers. Consider this excerpt from the essay "Products of Conception" which appears in the book "The Abortion Debate: TCU Voices" from 2012:

Nurse Bonnie L. McClory was an obstetric technician in the Labor and Delivery unit of what she calls a 'large metropolitan hospital.' She was pursuing a nursing degree and taking a class that would prepare her to work on the floor where babies were delivered. Sometimes the babies were delivered alive. Other times, the babies were delivered dead – the victims of saline abortions done at the hospital. A saline abortion is performed by sticking a needle into the woman's abdomen and injecting caustic saline solution into the amniotic fluid that surrounds her baby. This late-term abortion method uses the solution to poison the baby, who dies, sometimes over the course of several hours. Then labor is induced and the woman essentially 'gives birth' to a dead child. Sometimes babies were born alive after this technique. The problem of live births, as well as the risks to the mother from the saline injection, led to this method being abandoned by most abortionists in the 1990s.

McClory describes how she was the only pro-lifer in the class:

My status in the class was one of the maverick. I was staunchly pro-life; my views arose from my own experience of being un-intentionally pregnant at 17 and a mother at 18. None of my classmates had ever borne a child; only one was married. My classmates did not seem too affected by our having to watch a first trimester abortion from the operating room gallery as part of our training. I sat among them, tears staining my white scrub dress; they chatted about the handsome resident doing the procedure and how lucky the teenage patient was to be able to get on with her life. I fought nausea as I watched that handsome resident piece together what he had removed from the teenager's uterus as he made sure he got it all out. My classmates turned away from the sight of the little mound of red flesh laid out in the small metal basin. They turned away from my obvious grief, as well.

McClory was deeply saddened by her classmates' callous attitudes. Later, the OB techs were given the task of helping with saline abortions. McClory says

> *We OB techs were supposed to provide the supportive care to these [saline] patients while they labored and assist the doctor when he or she delivered the dead fetus. None of my OB Tech colleagues liked this part of the job. I heard them rationalize it, though, as a woman's right to choose. But it broke my heart, every time the doctor handed me a basin with a small, perfectly formed human baby lying dead and bloody inside it. I forced myself to rationalize that I had done nothing to bring about this death; I was merely cleaning up the aftereffects. That way, I could live with myself...*

McClory struggled with her conscience as her job required her to attend more and more abortions:

> *Saline abortions became more and more frequent in the Labor and Delivery Unit. In an effort to cope, I read about the procedure, hoping against hope that it was not as horrible as my mind imagined it to be. It wasn't – it was worse. The physician first raised a skin wheal with a local anesthetic on the maternal abdomen. Then a long needle was inserted into the uterus, through the numbed abdominal area. A fairly large amount of amniotic fluid was withdrawn from the uterus and then replaced with hypertonic saline. Hypertonic saline causes the fetal cells to burst. Death ensued shortly, but not before the fetus convulsed in death throes.*

Sometimes the mothers could feel these convulsions, depending on how far along in pregnancy they were.

She describes one horrific "delivery":

The doctors usually attended the saline abortion deliveries, which could be complicated. Many of the fetuses were born feet first. Delivering the small head could be challenging because the opening of the uterus, the cervix, sometimes closed down around the head, trapping it. Once I saw a doctor pull so hard, he detached the body from the trapped head. Of course, the fetus was already dead, but he was as horrified as I was; I saw his eyes above his blue facemask.

Most of the patients were heavily sedated; they were barely aware when their dead baby was whisked away in a basin. A few, however, were awake: The few patients who refused sedation had varying responses to their abortions, but most became agitated, a few hysterical. Some asked the sex of the aborted fetus. All of them looked away from the towel covered basin containing the dead baby.

McClory was given the task of handling the babies' bodies and preparing them to be sent to the pathology lab where they would be dissected:

Cleaning up meant boxing up the fetus in a round, white, one gallon cardboard container – the kind you see in ice cream stores. I had to place one of the mother's identification stickers on the box and then put it into the specimen refrigerator, awaiting its eventual destination in the pathology lab. At times I was the unwilling midwife, forced into delivering lifeless mites when I was the only one who walked into the labor room to find them half born.... I could also identify the gender of those fetuses; they were fully formed, even if they were only 5 to 8 inches long. I hated this part of my job...

But then there was the abortion that changed everything. Her assignment was to care for a teenager who went into labor after a saline abortion.

I remember looking at her chart, seeing the usual state required physician certification that the pregnancy was less than 20 weeks... I carried the usual little birth kit into her labor room; we did not bother to open a standard delivery room for an abortion patient. Before I had time to introduce myself, much less take her vital signs, it was obvious she was about to deliver. I hit the call button to summon help, opened the birth kit, donned my sterile gloves and proceeded to deliver a nearly 4-pound dead baby girl, about 15 inches long, with a full head of hair. I tried to hide the little body from the patient, she saw it, and began screaming. 'It's a baby! My baby! My baby!' When the doctor arrived, he brusquely told her to take the 'specimen' to the utility room. As she carried the baby away, the doctor injected the girl with a powerful narcotic and her screams died away into sobs. The baby was too big to fit into the containers that were generally used. Seeing this, the head nurse told McClory to get a baby shroud, and clean and dress the fetus for the morgue.

McClory describes the aborted baby girl:

She was beautiful, even in death. I gently cleaned her, patting her skin dry so it would not peel. Her silky fair hair had a slight curl to it after I washed it. She had long eyelashes, high cheekbones, and a tiny cleft in her chin. Her fingers were long and delicate, tiny nails dotting their ends. I picked up the necessary paperwork from the clerk and headed toward the back elevator. As I did so, I heard a woman asking the clerk if she could see her daughter. It was my patient's name she gave. A well-dressed couple in their mid-40s stood there. She had several diamond rings on her long fingers. He had fair, wavy hair and a cleft in his chin. Bile rose in my throat and it took every ounce of strength not to scream. The elevator came. I wheeled the little basin on board, pressed the button for the basement, and safely delivered her to the morgue....

Why had the girl been aborted so late? McClory soon found out:

On returning to the labor and delivery floor, my head nurse pulled me into her office to see if I was okay... I said, 'Nancy, how could that doctor mistake a nearly eight-month baby for an 18 weeker?

Even I can tell the difference when I palpate a pregnant abdomen.' Her eyes were damp, like she was going to cry. 'He knew right well she was that far long. Her parents are friends of his. Don't say another word. It will all come out in the wash. I knew she meant it would end up in the physicians' internal review committee, where doctors slapped each other on the wrist when they made mistakes that did not end up in litigation. I also knew the review committee was just a formality and that nothing would be done . . .

At the end of her shift, McClory submitted her resignation. Gone were the rationalizations. She could no longer aid in performing abortions, even if she was only "cleaning up" after them. McClory went on to raise her children and helped women facing unplanned pregnancies. As a nurse, she always refused to work in any clinic or hospital that did abortions. Her choice not to work in some facilities cost her job advancement opportunities and earned her the scorn of some of her colleagues. But she never again was involved in an abortion.[36]

Chapter 5–A Two-Pronged Approach

One's life has value so long as one attributes value to the life of others, by means of love, friendship, indignation and compassion.–Simone de Beauvoir

The pro-life movement is composed of two components that are both vital for the creation of a society that values each individual life, from the moment of conception to natural death. So far we have dealt with information and arguments supporting change; the changing of hearts, minds, and culture, and the changing of anti-life laws. Abby Johnson, the former Planned Parenthood employee who is now one of the leading voices in the country defending life, spoke out about change: "If we are able to make abortion illegal in the U.S., that's fine, but what we should strive for is to make it unthinkable."

The other leg of the pro-life movement is one that might be called "humanitarian". These are ground-roots efforts, most often local and nonprofit, that help women with the practical day-to-day needs in their emergency situations. These are the crisis pregnancy centers, also called CPCs, or pregnancy resource centers, of which there are approximately 2,752 in the United States, according to Pregnancy Help News. These centers are supported by almost 82,000 volunteers. Most often they provide counseling, adoption referrals, child rearing resources, job counseling, parenting classes, clothing, diapers, legal support, emergency and long-term housing, financial assistance, medical services, STD screenings, etc. Sixty percent of these centers offer free ultrasounds. While 11 states offer very limited financial support to these centers, none of them receive federal funds, unlike Planned Parenthood, which receives hundreds of millions of federal tax dollars every year. At least 90% of CPC funding comes via donations from local communities, and nearly 91% of clients report the highest level of satisfaction with the services they received.[37]

As might be suspected, Planned Parenthood continuously attacks CPCs, both defaming them with unproven allegations of almost everything imaginable, including lying, misleading women, performing illegal medical procedures, etc. PCPs have had to defend themselves from several expensive legal claims in the courts brought by Planned Parenthood. Apparently, Planned Parenthood would rather enrich themselves by aborting the babies of girls and women in desperate situations than allow anyone to help them with the practicalities of choosing life. Wikipedia's description of CPCs is equally vengeful, painting a subjective, negative image of CPCs as extremist zealots of the religious right.

In comparison, these centers have been the tiny humanitarian response to Planned Parenthood and other abortion providers for many years. Advertising doesn't comprise a large part of their budget, so they often struggle to make young women aware that they exist.

How effective are CPCs versus Planned Parenthood and other abortionists? Live Action, a national pro-life advocacy group, says that CPCs helped approximately 300,000 young women choose life for their children in 2015[38] while the Guttmacher Institute, Planned Parenthood's research and statistic division, claimed that there were approximately 926,200 abortions in the U.S. in 2014.[2] Using these statistics to describe CPCs effectiveness could lead to different conclusions. While the worth of 300,000 lives is immeasurable, more than three in every four women facing a crisis pregnancy are bypassing the CPCs in favor of abortion. Many women say they resorted to abortion because they didn't know where to find resources to help them in their situation. A 2018 survey by Andrea Pfarr in FemCatholic entitled "What Women Considering Abortion Need" reveals some frustrating responses.

> FemCatholic recently asked for responses to an anonymous survey about women's experiences with abortion. We wanted to listen to women and learn *from them* how we can better support women facing unexpected or challenging pregnancies. Some women talked about their own abortions. Some women (and two men!) shared about the abortion of someone very close to them. Below are the questions we asked and several of the responses we received. The comments were edited only for anonymity, length, and clarity (where needed). May we listen.
>
> ***What do you think was needed before the abortion? Please be as specific as possible. What resources or support was available? Would any other resources or specific support have changed the choice that was made?*** Several themes emerged among the responses to this question:

1. No one told her it was possible to have the baby, or showed confidence in her ability to be a mom.

'Being told I was strong enough to be a mom... I had no support. Not a single person around me told me it would be ok to have the baby. No one showed any confidence in me.'

'Things in society and culture telling young girls that they COULD raise a baby. Everything pointed/points to choosing abortion because of poverty, being single, being in high school, not being able to give a child a good life, it's too hard, you will be shunned, you won't have help, you'll live off the government forever, no one will want you anymore. It was very widespread that not having a baby at 18 was best for everyone.'

2. She did not know about resources.

'Needed: Practical resources, inspiration, and information. How can I finish my degree and be a parent? Where can I live? Can I continue in dorm housing? Are there other mothers out there with thriving careers who started out with an unplanned pregnancy as a single woman? Mentorship. Real live help, not a website or a call line.'

'After my abortion, I found out that there was special housing and financial aid at my college for 'non-traditional' students that would have been available to me. I also could have completed my degree in a modified way. It makes me sick to think about it. If that information had been readily available, I would have a ten year-old today.'

'My sister chose abortion because she could not see how she could get through law school with a baby. She said it was the hardest decision she had ever had to make, and she would not choose abortion again. If only she had had some reasonable way to help her finish law school with her baby! Daycare would have helped. Scholarships for people with crisis pregnancies would have helped. So would friends who actually favored a choice, not this awful 'choice'.

'More education on fetal development. Less lies— they said it was just a blob of tissue and not a human life. An ultrasound that I was allowed to see. Less hate towards someone considering it especially if they don't know any other options. Less hateful picketing at clinics and now social media.'

'In my tiny town the only resources available was at the health department with a hateful nurse and junk provided by Planned Parenthood. This is why I now volunteer at crisis pregnancy clinics. I wish I had gotten help for my alcohol problems which I believe strongly contributed to the first abortion.'

'When you go into the clinic they lie to you about fetal development and then they give you Valium or other conscious sedation while you wait. You are too high to stop it at that point.'

3. Parents were not supportive.

'I had no support. My boyfriend at the time was supporting and paid for the abortion. I believed the lies of the culture that abortion was the most responsible decision for a young woman in college to make. I didn't want an abortion... I needed family and friends who would forgive my mistakes and accept me for who I was then. I experienced no unconditional love until I met my husband now.'

'Having parents who would have understood a pregnancy outside of wedlock. The biggest (though not only) reason she got an abortion was that she couldn't handle telling her parents. I even spoke with their priest because I [the boyfriend] was against the abortion, and when I told him who they were (he didn't know me), he understood why my girlfriend at the time chose an abortion. He didn't endorse the choice, but he understood entirely.'

'I did not have any support. I come from a very, very traditional family. I felt so lonesome, scared. I knew my parents would kick me out of the house, and my partner ran away.'

'About changing my choice, if I had someone's support or understanding from my parents, I think I would not have done it.'

4. Chastity/abstinence messaging contributed to feelings of shame, a perceived lack of options, and fear.

'Familial support and a more pastoral response from the Church. My sister felt it was her only option because my mom had always been so vocal about not having sex until marriage and how sinful sex was. I don't think any of the chastity talks we attended helped in that regard either since they were mostly fear based tactics. She was terrified of being kicked out of my family, plus she was still in college and felt her abortion was the only way she'd be able to finish school. She didn't love the baby's dad and was also afraid my parents would make her marry him. It was so multifaceted but all based in extreme terror. I wish she had known about other pregnancy resource centers besides Planned Parenthood because they were all too willing to take her in and confirm her fear that her only option was abortion. But more than that, I think we need a cultural shift in how we speak about sex and pregnancy so that women in these positions don't feel so ostracized and shamed into trying to undo the situation without anyone knowing. The options shouldn't be to keep it all a secret or feel like a whore. When I asked her about adoption, she said she couldn't have lived 9 months with that much shame and everyone knowing and thinking poorly of her. We need compassion and understanding to fix this.'

'I'm talking about multiple friends' abortions here, not just of my generation, but also of my mother's. We both attended all-girls Catholic schools (both in Brooklyn, NY 30 years apart) so the options were laid out as quietly terminate the pregnancy or be removed from school and essentially ruin your life. There were no available resources at our schools for expectant mothers who did not plan to abort. Nobody spoke about supporting a teenage mother. I don't know that their choices would have been different, but my mother and I have discussed this extensively and we both definitely felt right along with them at the time that abortion was the only acceptable option offered by our Catholic community.'

5. Circumstances were dire, and she felt she had no other choice.

'I never asked for resources or support because honestly, I don't think anything could have changed my decision given my state of mind at the time. No one could have made me want a relationship with the father, preserved my budding career (walking through a newsroom as a single woman with an unplanned pregnancy), or taken away my shame. At 21 years old, I really and truly was not capable of taking care of myself.'

'My best friend fell pregnant when she was 17 following an affair with an older married man who convinced her he was going to leave his wife. I don't believe that anything would have changed the choice she made, as she was so afraid of the consequences of keeping the baby that far outweighed any other possible choices. She didn't tell anyone except for me. The man she had been with told her she couldn't keep the baby and took her to the clinic himself. Maybe having more support at clinics for these circumstances so that young women don't feel pushed or trapped in a situation. Holding men accountable too and not just making women take actions they later regret or possibly don't want to take in the first place.'

How are you or the woman close to you doing now? Have you/she sought any healing? What has helped? What still hurts?

The responses to this question fell into two categories: those that spoke of the lasting pain and trauma, and those that focus on healing.

1. The impact is lasting.

'It has been 20 years. I did go to confession and we worked through some stuff. It still hurts. Clinic was horrible and made fun of me the whole time because I was crying.'

'I still think about my child every June (when s/he would have been born). I should get help. I just pray for healing.'

'For 20 years I suffered tremendously both physically and psychologically. I have a tilted cervix, several problems during subsequent pregnancies when I married, PCOS. I had panic attacks. I also have struggled with anxiety and depression.'

'When I made first confession in February of this year before the Easter vigil when I entered the church, I truly felt forgiven and whole. My priest told me to look up Dorothy Day. He was so loving and so merciful when I didn't deserve it.'

'The regret will always be there. Always.'

2. Healing and peace are possible.

'I have done some healing. I've never really discussed it openly before. I have four beautiful children and I do my best by them and that makes me feel less horrid.'

'I'm pretty good. I feel spiritually and physically healed. Confession and joining the church helped tremendously. What still hurts – I miss my kid. But now I have even more motivation to strive for heaven so I can meet my child!'

'She's doing well now but it took about a year to get over the worst of the hurt. She joined a post-abortive women's group, named her baby, asked the baby for forgiveness and promised to hug him in heaven. She finally told me about a month after the fact and said that was crucial in her healing because before she had kept the whole thing just to herself and was simply tortured by it. She also promised the baby that she'd live a life that made her abortion worthwhile (debatable terminology but you get what she means), so she stopped the partying and sleeping with guys she didn't love and focused on school and making a life her baby would be proud of. Now she's graduating college with a good job and on a good path. I don't know what still hurts for her, we don't talk about it much. I think she's just trying to put it all behind her.'

'Talking to a Catholic therapist and a priest many years later (15+ years) definitely helped. They led me back to the sacraments, which has made all the difference. They tried to get me interested in healing retreats but I was never interested in mourning. My feeling was that the retreat would minimize or completely ignore the situation that led to my decision.'

'I am doing fine now. I had to find healing on my own and I found it after attending a Rachel's Vineyard retreat. What still hurts is knowing the people that pushed me (demanded) into the abortion have never apologized to me for their actions, words, and effectively, their lack of trust in me.'[39]

Kathleen Eaton-Bravo is one of the leading experts in the humanitarian response to the abortion crisis. Having been a successful businesswoman in the "for profit" world and working in the pro-life area for over 35 years, she has researched, launched and lead several CPCs, and now has created Obria, a successful, branded, nationwide alternative to Planned Parenthood. Describing the enormity of the abortion giant and how they ruthlessly and aggressively promote abortions, Kathleen believes the pro-life movement must watch them carefully and play their game. In no arena is this more important, she states, than in the area of technology, where Planned Parenthood now offers "dial-up abortions":

I was running three pregnancy centers and I'm looking at Planned Parenthood, and bottom line, we'd sit there all day and we'd pray and we'd talk and we'd pray, and the phone would ring and it was the wrong number . . . there's something wrong with a model where we sit and wait for the phone to ring, and by the way, we have to wait till she gets in a crisis pregnancy before we react. So . . . we've created this model, this faith-based lovely pro-life model, and we're saying we're going to let you go down the slippery slope,

70

we're going to let you get pregnant and we're going to hope you find us, . . .

It just has a problem where we sit and wait, we miss probably 98% of them, we catch one, we save the baby, and we count. I'm not dissing the . . . pregnancy resource centers. We were compassionate, we had heart, we loved, but God brought me into this ministry as a business-woman that realized that we can do better than this. So we actually looked at, and I've stuck with it all along, compassionate health care, empowering women, and changing lives. . . .

I hit the ground running . . . by the end of 2004 the three pregnancy centers were fully licensed medical clinics, moving toward a comprehensive, compassionate, holistic women's health care model. So what do we do today? We do pregnancy tests, ultrasounds, well woman care, pap smears, cancer screenings, UTI testing, we can do blood draws if she's having other problems, our staff is FEM trained . . .

We went "upstream". We became a proactive model instead of a reactive model. In other words, if I can get them off that slippery slope of hooking up and feeling that they won't have consequences, of buying into the secular world and society today, we have an opportunity to change (no matter what Planned Parenthood says), the world. We have an opportunity in women's health care, to be the players in the field, not

Planned Parenthood, because of . . . what we're doing in our clinics. So I don't need to be across the street from Planned Parenthood. I just have to have a comprehensive women's healthcare clinic that I can get them out of their clinic and into ours. Because I promise you, if they come into an Obria clinic, they never go back.

If we create a competitive model and get them out of Planned Parenthood, we're not only going to change their lives, we're also going to save babies, but we're not going to be counting them. Because we're going to get them off that slippery slope before they end up in a crisis pregnancy. . . I went into it to approach it from a business model, a competitive model, where we're In-n-Out, and they're McDonalds. And they're never going back to McDonalds. So I started doing this and we expanded our clinics in Southern California, and life kept changing.

And then what happened? I met an 84 year-old man who said 'Kathleen, I believe in taking your model national, but I'm 84 years old, and I want a return on my investment.' And so, it's going to take you a long time to convince the pro-life movement to move over from a pregnancy center model that's been entrenched here for 45 years, in which they're beautiful and they're lovely. I would say probably 90% of the pro-life groups out there are a pregnancy center with an ultrasound.

Now, say I'm a young woman and I want to go somewhere, and look up a pregnancy center . . . Planned Parenthood in the public schools has taught them if it's got 'life' in it (the title), if it's got 'options' in it, if it's got 'choice' in it, (it's a pro-life center) . . . if a girl is looking for an abortion, she's not going to go to a 'life center', she's going to go to Planned Parenthood, so we sort of shook up the model. I said if we're going to do this, we have to rebrand with a new name. Millennials want one word, one syllable and they can remember it. Think about it, everything, even Uber, is one word, very easy. So people said to me, 'What does Obria mean?' You have a little donor, a woman who has donated to us for 30 years and she says to us 'I love *Birth Choice*'. I said 'I know you do Honey. We were marketing you. But the problem is you were giving your money, but we weren't seeing any patients.' Because the pro-life movement markets the donors because we need money, but we've never moved over to understand we need to meet them (women) where they're at.

So we did focus groups at universities, we hired the students, we went out there, we did Birth Choice. Guess what? 87% said 'I know exactly what it is, I'm not going there.' In fact, the Charlotte Lozier Institute did a survey, and the survey numbers were pretty distressing. They went to university campuses and it was really interesting to see that 97% had never heard of Heartbeat, the Option Line, etc. They knew about pregnancy centers, but they would never go there, cause they already knew what they did. . . .

We hired a branding company and asked for 10 words. The word at the top was Obria . . . the bottom line is, I needed something I could own and trademark. We trademarked it nationally and internationally, we own it and guess what we're doing now? We are defining it. Nobody else is defining it, we are defining it. And so now Obria is in 8 states.

Now I'm going to take you into the world of today. . . an article that came out in November, 2016, said 'Abortion by prescription now rivals surgery for U.S. women.' Chemical abortions, the abortion pill. I'm not just talking about . . . Plan B . . . I'm talking about RU46. In Europe, RU46 has been out there many, many years, and right now 98% of first trimester abortions in Europe are done by the abortion pill. . . . 50% of the first trimester abortions in this country are done by the abortion pill.

Do you know what that means? That means she takes the first set of pills, and that kills the baby. In 72 hours she takes a series of pills, and those pills force her to abort the baby . . . she's in her bedroom most of the time, she goes in the bathroom, she aborts the baby and then what does she do? She picks the baby up and she flushes it down the toilet.

So, all that stuff I told you about how beautiful Obria is doesn't really mean anything anymore, because we were going from a pregnancy test to an ultrasound with a comprehensive women's healthcare clinic. The abortion pill became huge in our country... Planned Parenthood began dispensing the abortion pill through telemedicine. Telemedicine is an online virtual medical clinic. So this is it today. If you leave with nothing else, I need you to understand something. Today, the abortion is right here (holds up her phone). This is the abortionist, this is the abortion provider, this is the pill provider. The girl accesses it on an app on her smartphone, she takes the pill at home, she aborts in her bedroom while mom and dad are at work. This (the smartphone) is the abortion clinic of today.... Pregnancy resource centers, with pregnancy tests and ultrasound in a brick and mortar are great and even a mobile clinic. But here (the phone) is where they are. Telemedicine is an app that is a virtual medical clinic 24/7, it's called Planned Parenthood Direct. They man it with a nurse practitioner. The girl calls in, she fills out the patient intake form, pushes send, it goes into them (Planned Parenthood), they contact her and within 24 hours that girl has taken that pill. She's not even going into a Planned Parenthood. She's certainly not going to come into a pregnancy center with an ultrasound. She doesn't need an ultrasound.

Then Chuck Donovan from the Charlotte Lozier Institute called me and said ... we've discovered in our research there are 86 illegal sites dispensing RU46 from India and Thailand with no verification of pregnancy. A girl doesn't know she's on an illegal site. They're also selling them to drug dealers and they are now becoming one of the top drugs being sold on street corners, like opioids. In the community of Garden Grove (CA) ... it has reached epidemic levels.

I'm telling you this because we have to understand what we're facing today. And we have to understand our young girls, junior high, high school, and into college, they know they have 10 weeks to take that pill. So where are we? When I met that 84 year-old man and he told me about telemedicine, I didn't know what it was and I didn't care. All I knew was I wasn't starting anything else ... All this time I had been praying, knowing that the abortion pill is coming, and I knew what that meant. And I would pray 'God how are we going to reach them if they're aborting in their bedrooms?' .... I can tell you it took a year and over a million dollars. The technology changes all the time. Remember Planned Parenthood Direct? We're Obria Direct. We're down right now because we're doing GPS so we can drop it into any zip code anywhere in the country. 87% of millennials said they will not call a clinic. If they cannot schedule their appointment online, they're not going. So Planned Parenthood's telemedicine of course is connected, it's integrated into their website so when they pick up their phone and search for Planned

Parenthood, they fill out their application and guess what comes up? Boom. Here's the days, pick your appointment, tell us what you want, we got your appointment, we'll see you, and on the morning of the appointment, they send them a notice. That is electronic patient. . . . but in the pro-life movement you have to go and look at the pregnancy centers over here with their ultra-sounds and we're sitting here waiting, and all of a sudden everything is way over there . . . . now we're not going to get them, we can't touch them because of technology we don't have. And now we do. So our app will be online scheduling, it's being integrated into the website.

The other thing is this, how many websites do you think Planned Parenthood has for their 600 affiliates around the country? One. All 600 affil-iates are on one website. I was in Houston and I started searching. Do you know how many preg-nancy centers are in the greater Houston area? Twenty-two. How many websites were there? Twenty-two. You know where I'm going? So you've got this monstrous Planned Parenthood and it's damned good, it is. And then you've got these little pregnancy centers that don't have any money. They put no money in Google advertising. The first thing I ask when I go into a pregnancy center is 'How much money do you spend on Google ad words? How much money do you spend on your patient marketing program a month?' . . . How are they reaching them? Where do they go to find it? Where are they searching? And who is sending them there? Google. Google ad words. If you're not marketing on Google and you're not paying for Google ad words, and you're not optimizing your website and you're not doing all the fancy words out there to get them in to end up on your site, we're not going to win.

So of course then we had to move beyond that and say ok, we're hiring experts . . . we have a team of national patient marketing people with 10 landing pages on one Obria.org patient website. Every affiliate that comes on board gets their landing pages. So when a girl searches on Google and she comes up to Obria.org, it gets picked up by GPS and sends her directly to the landing pages of the clinic in her community. And we are ready to rock and roll. So when our telemedicine app comes back up, they can schedule their appointment, it's GPS. We put all our financing into one patient website: Obria.org. . . . and the next step is telemedicine. Because that's where she finds the abortion clinic and the abortion pill. And now she finds Obria Direct. We're connecting it to our website, it's seamless. . . . For every Obria clinic that opens up . . . they have telemedicine because this is where they need to be. Most importantly, it's one brand, and it's a proactive brand that goes upstream, it goes to colleges and universities, we market it, we advertise it, we bring them in, and now guess what? We're finally competing nose to nose with Planned Parenthood.[40]

Whatever outcome the woman eventually chooses for her baby, crisis pregnancies are fraught with fear, anxiety, panic, hopelessness, remorse, and desperation. Whatever the methods CPCs use to help women and girls in problem pregnancies, the most important ingredient is compassion, and that is the specialty of the CPCs. A firm, informed, unflinching response to abortion is necessary when confronting anti-life politicians who celebrate the passage of abortion-till-birth laws, Planned Parenthood, other abortionists and promoters of abortion. However, the women and girls who are facing desperate situations need the kind, understanding and nonjudgmental concern that will help them to realize they have alternatives to abortion.

Societal norms change over time. We might be changing from what happened years ago: looking down on and whispering about a teenager being pregnant, to looking at that girl who decides to have her baby with admiration and a desire to help.

Post abortive women who regret their abortions, and suffer physically, mentally, and emotionally from them, should receive our compassion and support. The post-abortive women who conquer their anguish by becoming pro-life advocates are the best resources we have for changing the hearts and minds of those who have no problem killing unborn human life.

Those who are forced or deceived into having an abortion against their will also need an equal amount of compassion and help with their healing. Similar to the CPCs that help women before delivery, there exist several organizations that are devoted to helping remorseful and emotionally troubled women heal from their abortion, such as Project Rachel (Rachel's Vineyard), Healing Pathways, Exhale, Option Line, Abortion Changes You, Hope After Abortions, National Office of Post-Abortion Reconciliation and Healing, and Support After Abortion.

A story worth reading is in Abby Johnson's book "*Un*planned". Ms. Johnson had a lucrative career as a clinic manager at a very large Planned Parenthood facility in Texas and had two abortions herself. She had been taught by Planned Parenthood to counsel women by assuring them that they were pregnant with just a blob of tissue. In September, 2009, she was asked to assist for the first time in the abortion of a 13-week preborn baby. It turned out to be a completely life changing event for her. After watching in horror on the ultrasound at the baby first squirming to avoid the suction tube, then fighting it, then being sucked into it in pieces, she had such a violent emotional and physical reaction, she immediately typed up her resignation and never went back. She is now one of the leading figures in the pro-life movement. Her biographical film "Unplanned", which was released in theaters at the end of March, 2019 despite enormous opposition from the mainstream media, was a social phenomenon in that it was one of the first examples of a wide-release movie that is pro-life, and in the change it caused in the modern U.S. mindset on abortion. Consider these words by Ms. Johnson when she speaks of the two victims in an abortion:

> When I first left Planned Parenthood, I obviously had a lot to process. It was easy for me to see that I had a hand in taking the life of innocent children. Of course...I had seen one die in front of my eyes. These children were obviously the primary victims of abortion.

> But I kept hearing people in the pro-life movement talking about how women were secondary victims to abortions and that was really hard for me to swallow. Not because it was hard to understand, but because if I admitted that women were

the secondary victims to abortions, then I had to admit that I was a victimizer...a perpetrator. Was I really? I thought I was trying to help women.

Then God called to mind all of the times where women had come into my office, tearful, unsure of their decision and I had pressured them to abort...because I didn't want to take the time to properly go over their options. Or the times that Christian women came in asking me for counsel and I used my supposed Christianity to manipulate them into thinking God was perfectly fine with abortion. Or the times when a woman had said 'no' on the table, tried to get up and the nurse would give her another round of sedation to shut her up. I remember laughing when the doctor would say that they 'sedated her objections.' I remember hearing other workers talking about physically holding down women who tried to get off the table. And even the times when women were brought in by abusive parents, boyfriends, pimps...we asked no questions...we took their money and performed the abortion while these women were in tears.

Were women victims of abortions? Yes. They absolutely were. Were those of us who worked in these clinics abusers? Yes, we were.

So, just like everything else, I had to work through that. I had to make apologies. I had to ask God for forgiveness...and then I had to accept that forgiveness.

Anyone who thinks that women who abort aren't victims of the societal pressure to normalize abortion, or even the physical or emotional pressure to abort from those around them, are truly blind to what's happening...either blind or willfully ignorant. Even women who 'shout their abortions' are shouting out of hurt...sometimes it's hurt they haven't even begun to realize yet.

Because abortion isn't normal. No matter how many people try to say it is, it just isn't. It can never be normal for a mother to take the life of a child. It goes against our very inborn nature. Your life is never the same after you take innocent life.[41]

Chapter 6–Where have our morals, truth and priorities gone?

Our lives begin to end the day we become silent about things that matter.- Martin Luther King, Jr.

C onspicuously absent from the anti-life side of the debate is an examination of our social priorities. It has become very inconvenient in the United States to examine our conscious, both collectively and individually. George Washington's honesty in admitting to chopping down the cherry tree, whether true or fictitious, has always been held up as one example of the positive values that have been interwoven in the collective social and moral fabric of our country since its inception. Concepts such as acknowledging and taking responsibility for one's actions have been the moral compass of our culture and society for centuries. Obviously, those in the public eye have not always exercised good moral judgment, but the American people could always clearly see the path that would lead to higher moral ground and lofty goals.

We now find ourselves as a society set adrift in the confusing crosscurrents of what is acceptable and what is not. Our children see sports figures, musicians and actors they idolize abusing drugs and alcohol, using steroids, and engaging in all sorts of illegal activities. Little wonder that we have become desensitized to these infractions. Scandal is hardly scandalous any longer. A president who engaged in sexual activities with someone other than his spouse in the Oval Office modeled for us how to spin the story, lie, and squirm out of responsibility. He now takes his place among the "best" and "most respected" presidents in public opinion polls, and earns millions of dollars in speaking engagements.

Unfortunately, personal improprieties by politicians are commonplace today, and as some would argue, they always have been. What then, is different? The difference is that in approximately the last forty years, we have conveniently convinced ourselves that shame and guilt should be purged from our society. Recent psychological and child rearing fads teach us that shame and guilt are taboo. No one, child or adult, should ever feel bad for what they've done, which begs the question: How do we know or learn what is inappropriate behavior when the boundaries have disappeared?

On March 21, 2019, Monsignor Stuart Swetland gave some insights on guilt on his Relevant Radio broadcast, "Go Ask Your Father."

> Guilt is good. Just like pain is good. If I go running or exercising and begin to feel intense pain . . . that's healthy, because it's telling me something's wrong. If I keep exercising or running, I might do real damage. That pain is what a healthy organism has to signal to us that something is off, something is wrong. . . .
>
> In a similar way, in the moral realm, when we have done something that is objectively wrong, we should feel guilty. If we do something that is objectively wrong, and we don't feel guilt, that is

highly problematic. Just like a physical organism that would never feel pain, that would be a real danger to that organism's survival and ability to thrive because all kinds of harm could come to someone who didn't feel pain when something was wrong. If I put my hand on a hot stove and didn't feel pain, that would be a real problem. I could do real damage to my hand. In a similar way, to do something wrong and not feel guilty about it, in the technical sense, if you absolutely never feel guilt about any wrongdoing, that makes you a sociopath or a psychopath . . . .

So guilt, properly understood, is good. It motivates us, it moves us to do good, and to repent from any wrongdoing that we have done. And in that, we should be thankful for guilt, because it means we have a healthy conscience that motivates us to overcome that weakness or that immorality. Much like an athlete who falls short of his or her goals is motivated to work harder to reach those athletic goals or endeavors. A person who's trying to live an upright and holy life, when they have done something that is wrong, should feel and experience guilt to motivate them to overcome that sin.

Passage of Roe vs. Wade would have been unimaginable before the values shift of the sexual/social revolution of the 1960's. The legalization of tearing pieces of a living unborn fetus from his mother's womb would have resulted in upheaval and clamoring dissent by the American public. But once the values drift began and our moral compass became disabled, the pro-death advocates realized that their time had come. "Personal freedom" was the mantra as we cast off the restrictions of shame and guilt for wrongdoing. "You have to decide what is right for you." This convenient "get out of jail free" card of moral relativism has created the idea that each individual can create his or her own version of truth and reality; a reality that fits each individual's lifestyle, free of any kind of boundaries or consequence. Collective and long standing norms that have served as guidelines and pillars supporting the moral fabric of cultures for millennia were destroyed in a few decades in favor of a philosophy that permits the individual to do as he or she pleases, without any thought for the greater good of others.

The question "What is truth?" is perhaps one of the oldest philosophical questions in history. Thousands of philosophers throughout history have tried to find a definition for "truth". However, three words that often appear in definitions of truth are "fact", "reality", and "knowledge."

If we look at what is the reality of the facts regarding abortion, we can't ignore that the unborn is a living organism. By definition, living things grow and change. If left undisturbed, the fertilized human egg will grow and change into a completely formed, functioning, living baby. We also know that the parents that supplied the genes for this individual were human beings, therefore, the offspring is also human. Additionally, we also know that abortion is an act that results in the destruction of this living human being. If it didn't, after 40 weeks, the outcome would be a living human baby.

Whatever the argument may be, real truths are not up for debate. They are not relative. They have stood the test of time for millennia, since ancient Greek and Roman times and before. Individual manipulation of the truth creates as many potential "truths" as there are humans on earth. American philosopher

Dallas Willard said, "The bitterness of truth is its total indifference to human will and desire, together with the fact that human desire and will are set on reshaping reality and therefore truth to suit itself."

Truths can be difficult to accept. Truths can be inconvenient. Truths can be painful. You can try to refute them. You can try to manipulate them. You can ignore them. But truths are everlasting. They can be beautiful and insightful. They do not change, and haven't changed for millennia. Since the dawn of humanity, the truth that murder is wrong has been irrefutable. That truth became negotiable with the passage of Roe v. Wade. Universal concepts of "right" and "wrong" have been the rock and foundation that has steadied world cultures for millennia. When we start changing and compromising these truths for our own comfort and convenience, we cut the ties of social and cultural stability that set us adrift in a sea of chaos, confusion, division, violence, and eventually, self-destruction.

To be sure, many decisions one must make regarding his or her own life need to take into account each individual's situation and circumstances. However, the "do whatever is right for you" philosophy has caused us to jump one step further to include the addendum "at all cost, and if necessary, without consideration of others or the common good." The dangers of this moral relativism have been sorely underestimated.

We hear liberal politicians take the Pope to task for not being more "progressive" and not "adapting to the times." Narcissistic, arrogant politicians feel entitled to lecture the church on what it should believe and teach. They admonish that the church needs to "catch up with the times" and sanction a woman's right to kill her unborn human life, or as they put it "not deny women their 'reproductive rights'". However, it's not the church's job to conform to the latest moral issues dictated by what is socially in vogue at the time. The church has existed for over 2,000 years as a consistent beacon of values that guide, anchor, and nurture humanity and culture.

But we worship at the altar of ego, instant gratification, comfort and convenience. Humility is a quaint relic. We won't allow our narcissistic selves to endure any sacrifice, convincing ourselves that we deserve a suffer-free life. What would our grandparents and great-grandparents think if they could see our obsession with comfort and convenience? The world as it existed 150 years ago demanded sacrifice, deprivation and delayed gratification. Some would say this environment forged the character and strength of our forefathers, which in turn forged our country as the leader of the world. Mainstream narcissism and craving of instant gratification and convenience have debased our culture into one of "I am entitled to have whatever I desire immediately, with a minimum of effort on my part, because I deserve it." When the national psyche has been groomed by the media and Wall Street to believe an individual is the center of the universe, it is easy to convince them that the result of their own actions, the creation of a human life and the work and responsibility that it requires, can easily be done away with.

An article in a book written by Paul Roberts entitled "The Impulse Society: America in the Age of Instant Gratification" appeared in the business section of the Los Angeles Times. It describes how Roberts feels that

> The market prevails because humans are evolutionarily unsuited to fend off profiteers competing to 'the highest level of momentary pleasure for the least effort' . . . The result is an insular, sad and fat America . . .Narcissism is rising – and, although this is 'suited to a corporate world,' it has hooked Americans into a cycle

of 'rapid self-gratification.' The housing bubble that ignited the Great Recession revealed a Wall Street-driven scheme to manipulate individual greed. The healthcare system . . . is at the mercy of pushy narcissists who are 'particularly unsuited to contemplating death.' They over-consume every expensive new treatment cooked up for profit.[42]

We also have become more "animalistic." As long as Hollywood glorifies people on screen having indiscriminate sex every ten minutes, there will continue to be unexpected pregnancies. For the last 45 years, we have been fed the image that it is glamorous to have random, casual, unprotected sex with the first person that comes along, as if this were the most popular, natural, normal and consequence-free thing to do; to have no more humanity, consciousness and self-control than other mammals. With no higher sense of principles and self awareness, humans can also sink to an animalistic level. At the very least, the sexual revolution of the 60's taught us that two unmarried people in a relationship automatically must be having sex. This has become as natural and expected as thunder following lightening.

Closer examination of our national psyche also reveals evidence of the skewed priorities that have become so commonplace they seem normal. One such "priority" is that we now value animal life more than human life. Marchers protesting the mistreatment of animals are generally viewed as advocating for the (animal) lives of those who cannot speak up to defend themselves. Pro-life marchers who advocate for the lives of those humans who cannot speak up to defend themselves are often reviled, harassed, and even jailed. Animal rights advocates establish shelters from where we can save dogs and cats by adopting them. Euthanizing these animals is seen as something to be avoided. Killing unborn humans is not.

On June 4, 2019, the same New York legislators who six months earlier celebrated the passing of one of the most extreme anti-life bills allowing abortions until birth passed another bill outlawing the declawing of cats. Animal welfare advocates called the procedure "cruel and barbaric."[43] Evidently murdering an unborn child by dismemberment or lethal injection isn't as "cruel and barbaric."

In 1940, the United States government passed the "Bald and Golden Eagle Protection Act" which declares it illegal to

> take, possess, sell, purchase, barter, offer to sell, transport, export or import, at any time or in any manner, any bald eagle commonly known as the American eagle, or any golden eagle, alive or dead, or any part, nest, or egg thereof of the foregoing eagles . . . [44]

How can the government extend legal protection to cats and unborn eagle babies inside the egg, while unborn humans no longer enjoy any legal protection from being killed? Where are our priorities? Where is our conscious?

Pro-life advocates look around at the sale of baby body parts, the harvesting of intact organs via abortion procedures that are illegally modified to deliver an intact baby sometimes born alive, the proposals to allow babies born alive from unsuccessful abortions to die while health care workers stand by waiting, doing nothing, and wonder in shock and desperation, "What has happened to us as a society? How did this nightmare become reality?" These are three possible explanations, all of them frightening reflections on our current culture and society:

First, as previously mentioned, we now live in an age where a new religion is replacing traditional theism: the worship of ego, comfort and convenience, greatly aided by technology.

Second, the disappearance of any sense of guilt, responsibility, or morality (concepts that go against comfort and convenience) and the growth of moral relativism, the idea you can create your own personal reality and truths to fit your comfort and convenience. Anti-lifers think they no longer must accept or believe proven scientific data and research if it doesn't fit their tightly held, but misguided narrative.

Third, a growing refusal or inability to acknowledge the humanity of the unborn, as well as the elderly and mentally challenged, in spite of scientific proof that these are all human beings, and because they are human beings, have inherit worth.

Since the passage of Roe v. Wade in 1973, the abortion debate has evolved. For the next 40 years, Planned Parenthood and other abortionists enjoyed a complacency that they had "won", and all they had to do was hide the truth about abortion from the public, because they knew it was gruesome, violent murder. They were very successful at keeping it off the national radar. It was ignored, rarely debated publicly, and while it operated in almost an underground fashion, it expanded and became entrenched. Planned Parenthood's campaign of disinformation kept it out of the public eye.

A chilling phase of the recent evolution of the abortion debate is that they now are beginning to publicly admit they know that the fetus is a living human life, and they are willing to kill it anyway. This growing misguided and dangerous cultural mindset can and must be corrected if our society is to survive. To correct it, we must educate ourselves and then educate others in regards to ethics, morals, and all the basic foundational principles that create and maintain a healthy culture and society. Your reading this book is the first step. The second step is much harder: engaging others in this crucial conversation.

There comes an important crossroad in most parents' lives that almost no parent is aware of. It's the point at which we unconsciously stop teaching our children about life, about right and wrong. All effective parents teach their toddlers to not hit others, to share, to cooperate, etc. As children grow, what they need to learn changes with their phase of intellectual development. Hopefully, as a pre-teen, your child has mastered not hitting others, sharing and cooperating fairly well, and are now ready for learning more mature concepts such as how to protect oneself, how to choose friends that will take you in a positive direction, etc. Teenagers are able to comprehend and appreciate learning about both practical and philosophical issues: how to drive a car, how to seek and obtain fulfillment in life, how to wisely choose a husband or wife, why it's important to respect human life, etc.

Enormous damage is done when parents reach that "I'm done parenting" threshold before the most complex and important concepts are taught. Some parents stop guiding and instructing their children at 12, for others 15 or 16, before they have formed their children with some of the most important teachings in life.

A concurrent phenomena is that once parental teaching is done, introducing or revisiting the untaught topics is taboo, for fear of causing disagreement. Heaven forbid should a parent cause any kind of discord in the family for trying to teach his or her 25 year-old that aborting your baby girl is not acceptable because you wanted a boy, or that harvesting organs from a baby that has been delivered prematurely and still has a beating heart is somehow unacceptable. This is "parental abdication", where the parents' goal is to become their child's friend and no longer their parent. In reality, these parents are enabling a new culture to emerge that has seriously run off the tracks. Learning is a lifelong endeavor, as is teaching. Wise parents know this. Wise (adult) children patiently hear it.

Chapter 7–Statistics and Politics

A single death is a tragedy, a million deaths are a statistic–attributed to Joseph Stalin.

O ver the years, abortion has become more and more a political issue, to the point where it now defines the former Democrat Party as their signature issue. "Former Democratic Party" because after the party's sudden stampede into extremist leftist politics, the majority of the party believes socialist philosophies are more beneficial to the United States.[45] Socialist/ democrat party chairman Tom Perez publicly announced that

> Every Democrat, like every American, should support a woman's right to make her own choices about her body and her health. That is not negotiable, and should not change city by city or state by state.[46]

Governor Andrew Cuomo also publicly stated that those who oppose abortion have "no place in the state of New York".[47] These statements immediately alienated the 23% of Democrats who think abortion should be illegal in virtually all circumstances.[46] It would seem that partisan politics demand that Socialists/Democrats do complex mental gymnastics to convince themselves that abortion is acceptable as a requirement for party membership. And the great majority of them blindly obey.

Abortion has also been a state issue, even prior to the Roe. V. Wade decision, meaning each individual state made its own legal policy regarding abortion. The passage of Roe v. Wade moved abortion more into the federal arena. Before Roe v. Wade, a handful of states had already legalized abortion under limited circumstances. Each state has created its own policies and standards regarding the details of the practice of abortion. The Guttmacher Institute, Planned Parenthood's research branch, has data for each state covering topics such as whether abortions must be performed by a licensed physician (42 states require it), when an abortion must be performed at a hospital, how abortions may be funded, insurance issues, if providers may refuse to participate, if pre-abortion counseling is required, what that counseling may contain, if there's a waiting period before obtaining an abortion, what is the required parental notification and involvement when minors seek an abortion, restrictions based on fetal age, if any, the legality of partial-birth abortions, is an ultrasound mandatory, etc. In reality, many legal restrictions on abortion are not enforced.

Statistics from public opinion polls in support or opposition of abortion are complicated and often contradictory. It is not uncommon to see anti-life organizations and the media armed with poll statistics in direct contrast to the statistics offered by the pro-life side on the same topic. Most of these discrepancies arise from how the survey questions are asked. For example, the question "Are you in favor of restrictions on abortion?" will yield different results than "Are you in favor of restricting a woman's right to make her own decisions regarding her reproductive health?" A question that includes the words "with no exceptions" usually skews the results heavily to the anti-life side.

Questions regarding partial birth abortions or third trimester abortions usually show a majority against these procedures.

Consequently, each side of the debate, especially the anti-life side, very carefully chooses the language used in their survey questions to produce results that are more desirable for them. They can then point to their own survey results to support their claim, for example, that the majority of Americans are in favor of abortion. Therefore, it is important to be aware of who has done the polling and how the questions are worded when looking at public opinion surveys. A careful and balanced review of polls on abortion going back to the '80s show that for the most part, the American public has been fairly evenly divided on the issue.

However, something very interesting happened in early 2019: a rapid legal division among states began to either solidify and expand the legality of abortion in state constitutions, or pass laws to protect unborn life. Politically liberal states had been uneasily watching the rise of pro-life legal victories in the 2010's. Conservative states began passing legislation such as The Pain Capable Unborn Children Protection Act, partial-birth abortion bans, informed consent laws, waiting periods, ultrasound laws, parent involvement laws, prohibitions of tax funded abortions, etc. After the videos of Planned Parenthood trafficking in baby body parts and other scandals came to light, these states began clamoring more loudly to defund the abortion giant. Melanie Israel is a research associate for the Heritage Foundation. In a February 21, 2019 report, she states

> In the past decade, states have enacted more than 300 laws that protect innocent human life. In response to this wave of significant pro-life victories, some state legislatures across the country are passing or considering sweeping

pro-abortion legislation that far exceeds *Roe v. Wade* and its progeny. These bills are radically out of step with the American people's consensus that abortion should be significantly restricted. While the bills in various states differ based on current state law, they have generally allowed for elective abortion up to birth, reduce or eliminate health and safety standards for clinics and practitioners, and end requirements to provide medical care to babies born alive following an abortion procedure.

In response to these radical proposals, members of the United States Congress are working to advance pro-life policies, including the Born Alive Abortion Survivors Protection Act, to protect women and their babies—born and unborn.

Current federal policy insufficiently protects babies who are born alive following an attempted abortion. While current law recognizes that all infants born alive are 'persons,' babies who survive an abortion attempt are left vulnerable because the law provides for no requirements that health care practitioners treat the infant with the same degree of care afforded to any other newborn. The Born-Alive Abortion Survivors Protection Act would remedy this problem by requiring that proper medical care be given to infants who survive an abortion and establishing criminal consequences for practitioners who fail to do so.[48]

It could be argued that the aforementioned pro-life legal victories and the fear of losing Roe vs. Wade drove politically liberal states to confirm and expand abortion in their state constitutions. What is clear is that in the mid and late 2010's, the former Democratic (now Socialist by their own admission) party experienced a very rapid and violent swing to the left. It was at this time they chose abortion as their signature political issue to celebrate, enshrine and defend at all costs. America was not prepared for this extremist position regarding abortion. Only five years earlier, the "pro-choice" plank of the party declared that abortion should be "safe, legal, and rare". That phrase was removed, and they now believe abortion should be promoted at all phases of pregnancy, for any or no reason, until birth. They claim that late term abortions would happen only in cases where the mother's physical or emotional health would be affected by having a baby. However, the term "emotional health" is so loosely interpreted, that in reality, a woman can get a third trimester abortion quite easily in places where it is legal. There was even a proposal in Virginia, defended by the leftist governor, that would have allowed abortion till the moment of delivery, and permitted a baby born alive after an unsuccessful abortion to be left to die.

The controversial decision of January 22, 2019, in which some New York politicians celebrated the legalization of abortion until the moment of birth with the lighting of One World Trade Center in pink lights, caused an uproar across the United States. But very quickly Rhode Island, Vermont, Illinois, and Massachusetts all began drafting similar legislation that would ensure abortion on demand until birth in the event that Roe was overturned. What many were unaware of was that late-term abortion had already been legal in Alaska, Colorado, New Hampshire, New Jersey, New Mexico, Oregon, Vermont, and the District of Columbia for many years. The de facto result of even just one state allowing abortion until birth is that anyone in the United States who can travel to that state can get a third trimester abortion, making it essentially available in the entire U.S.

This rush to embrace extreme, radical abortion laws had an interesting effect on the public's opinion of abortion, especially late term abortion. A Marist poll conducted in February, 2019 found that

> In just one month, Americans have made a sudden and dramatic shift away from the pro-choice position and toward a pro-life stance . . . The shift was led by Democrats and those under 45 years old, according to a survey taken Feb.12-17 in the wake of efforts in several states to legalize abortion up until birth.

> Current proposals that promote late-term abortion have reset the landscape and language on abortion in a pronounced – and very measurable – way, said Barbara Carvalho, director of The Marist Poll.

> In a substantial, double-digit shift, according to the poll, Americans are now as likely to identify as pro-life (47 percent) as pro-choice (47 percent). Just last month, a similar survey conducted by The Marist Poll found Americans more likely to identify as pro-choice than as pro-life by 17 percentage points (55 to 38 percent). Democrats moved in their pro-life identity from 20 percent to 34 percent. Among Democrats, the gap between pro-life and pro-choice identifiers was cut in half from 55 percent to 27 percent. The number of

Democrats now identifying as pro-life is 34 percent, up from 20 percent last month, while the number identifying as pro-choice fell from 75 percent to 61 percent. Younger Americans also moved dramatically, now dividing 47 percent pro-life to 48 percent pro-choice. One month ago, the gap was almost 40 percentage points with only 28 percent identifying as pro-life and 65 percent identifying as pro-choice.

This is the first time since 2009 that as many or more Americans have identified as pro-life as have identified as pro-choice. More than a third of Democrats (34 percent) as well as two-thirds of Republicans (67 percent) identify as pro-life. Independents divide (46 percent pro-life, 48 percent pro-choice).

At the same time, the survey found that opposition to late-term abortions is overwhelming. By about three to one (71 percent to 25 percent), Americans say abortion should be generally illegal during the third trimester. This majority includes 60 percent of Democrats, 72 percent of independents and 85 percent of Republicans.

By an even wider margin (71 percent to 18 percent), Americans strongly oppose late-term abortion after 20 weeks. This 71 percent includes two-thirds (66 percent) who say abortion should be banned after 20 weeks of pregnancy except to save the life of the mother. Only 18 percent think abortion should be allowed at any time up until birth. Those opposing abortion after 20 weeks, or overall, include: 59 percent of Democrats, 78 percent of independents, and 82 percent of Republicans.

In addition, the poll found that 80 percent of Americans would like abortion limited to – at most – the first three months of pregnancy, an increase of five points since just last month. This includes 65 percent of those who identified as pro-choice, as well as strong majorities of Democrats (64 percent), Republicans (92 percent) and independents (83 percent).[49]

Anti-life proponents promote another lie . . . that third trimester or late term abortions are very rare, and that those that do happen are a result of threats to the mother's health or severe fetal abnormalities. However, while specific numbers are hard to come by, most sources agree that approximately 14,000 late term abortions are done a year in the United States, and Planned Parenthood's own statistics show that almost none of these are carried out due to health concerns for the mother or abnormalities in the baby. According to the Charlotte Lozier Institute,

Defenders of late-term abortion frequently make the assertion that late-term abortions are 'almost always' carried out in cases of severe fetal abnormality or danger to the mother's life. Reporting on the results of a study of late-term abortions in 2013 (Foster, Kimport) in the journal Perspectives on Sexual and Reproductive Health, a publication of the pro-choice Guttmacher

Institute, the authors acknowledge that 'data suggests that most women seeking later terminations are not doing so for reasons of fetal anomaly or life endangerment.' Using interviews and questionnaires for women who had first trimester abortions versus second and third trimester abortions, the authors . . . found that the rationales cited by the two groups were essentially the same – stressful circumstances of unprepared pregnancy, single-motherhood, financial pressure, and relationship discord. . . . In an April 2018 report for the Congressional Research Service, Dr. Foster is cited as believing "that abortions for fetal anomaly 'make up a small minority of later abortion' and that those for life endangerment are even harder to characterize."[50]

The anti-life groups and the great majority of the current press would like us to believe that the only supporters of life are ultra conservative, right-wing evangelical Christians. Their private assumption is that this is an easily targeted group, and that by labeling them as "extremists" or "radicals", a culture war can be created in the United States, dividing and polarizing our society even further. Since we are living in an era of open hostility to religion, especially Christianity, this plays especially well into the hands of the pro-death supporters.

The facts, however, reveal otherwise. The Pew Research Center is a highly respected, nonpartisan research group founded in 2004, and is headquartered in Washington, D. C. It describes itself as "a 'fact tank' that provides information on the issues, attitudes and trends shaping America and the world." It "does not take positions on policy issues." The description of their code of ethics states that "Independence, impartiality, open-mindedness and professional integrity are indispensable to the mission and success of the Pew Research Center."

Research from the Pew Center shows that 24%, almost a full quarter of those they polled who described themselves as "unaffiliated" with any religion, feel that abortion should be illegal in most or all cases. In fact, their research shows support for abortion is dropping among almost all religious, socio-economic, racial, political and gender groups. From 2007/2008 to just a year later, support for keeping abortion legal among conservative and moderate democrats fell by 4%, and among liberal democrats, it fell by 5%. Among mainline protestants, support fell by 10%, among Catholics it fell 8%, while maintaining legality for abortion dropped 10% among Jews. Six percent fewer college graduates expressed support for keeping abortion legal, and in all geographic areas of the United States, support for abortion dropped between 5 and 8%. Total figures for all groups in the United States showed that keeping abortion legal had 7% fewer supporters, while 4% more favored making it illegal, in the space of less than two years.[51]

Gallup, one of the most well-known and respected polling organizations in the United States, conducted ten polls from May, 2009 through May, 2014. Results show that the percentages of people who self-identify as pro-choice and pro-life are almost even. This is in stark contrast to the disingenuous claim touted by pro-death supporters that "the majority of Americans are pro-choice." More interesting was the Gallup poll from May, 2013, that found that 31% of people identifying themselves as Democrats said they were pro-life.[52]The most recent annual Gallup poll on abortion, released in June, 2019 shows a slight but continued increase in the American public's support for life. Political scientist Dr. Michael J. New interprets these latest Gallup results.

According to the survey, a plurality of Americans now identify as pro-life, with 49 percent of respondents calling themselves 'pro-life,' and 46 percent calling themselves 'pro-choice.' This is the first Gallup poll since 2013 in which a higher percentage of respondents identified as 'pro-life' rather than 'pro-choice.'

The new survey also found that the percentage of Americans who think abortion should either be 'illegal in all circumstances' or 'legal in only a few circumstances' increased from 53 to 60 percent between 2018 and 2019. A Gallup poll conducted in May, meanwhile, found that the percentage of Americans who consider abortion immoral reached 50 percent for the first time since 2012.

This gain in public support for the pro-life position is more significant than many observers realize. There is some evidence that pro-life sentiment tends to wane during Republican presidential administrations, as well as when abortion opponents are poised to make substantial policy gains. Some pro-life observers have been concerned that efforts to enact abortion limitations in Alabama, Georgia, Missouri, and a handful of other states might result in a public-opinion backlash. This new Gallup poll illustrates that this likely has not been the case. In fact, it is entirely possible that aggressive efforts by Democrats to make abortion policy more permissive in states such as New York, Vermont, and

Illinois actually might have resulted in gains in pro-life sentiment.

Americans' attitudes on abortion and other life issues inevitably fluctuate from year to year, which is why it's important to remember the long-term gains the pro-life movement has made in public-opinion polling over time. In 1995, Gallup found that only 33 percent of Americans identified as 'pro-life,' but since 1997, pro-life sentiment has reached at least 40 percent in every Gallup poll. In both 2009 and 2012, majorities of respondents to Gallup's survey identified as 'pro-life,' and pro-life efforts to educate the public likely have been an essential reason why the U.S. abortion rate has declined by more than 50 percent since 1980.[53]

Still another nationwide survey of women conducted by the Center for Gender Equality, run by former Planned Parenthood President Faye Wattleton revealed that a majority of women (51%) believe abortion should either never be permitted or permitted only for rape, incest, or life endangerment.[54] That means a majority of women believe abortion should be permitted only in extremely rare circumstances. (Rape/incest abortions account for only 1% of abortions every year according to the Guttmacher Institute, discussed below, and life-saving abortions are similarly rare.)[55]

On March 23, 2015, *USA TODAY* columnist and associate professor at Fordham University, Charles Camosy, in an article titled "Millennials Will Change Abortion Conversation", wrote that, while not in favor of making abortion illegal in all cases,

The conventional wisdom is that young people are strongly pro-choice. While it is not surprising that Baby Boomers and Gen Xers eventually grew more skeptical over time, when they were teenagers and young adults, they too were all-in for abortion rights. But the demographic future of the United States is defying that conventional wisdom. Gallup found in 2010 that 'support for making abortion broadly illegal (was) growing fastest among young adults.' Oh, and remember the debate in Texas and the U.S. House about banning abortion beyond 20 weeks? According to the *National Journal*, 44% of those 50 and older supported such a ban, compared with 52% of those ages 18-29.Perhaps even more telling than these polls are the reactions of abortion-rights advocacy groups such as Emily's List and NARAL Pro-Choice America. They are very publicly worried about something former NARAL president Nancy Keenan called the 'intensity gap.' Of young people who identify as 'pro-life,' for instance, 51% claim that abortion is an important issue. But for young people who identify as 'pro-choice,' that percentage plummets to 20%. Fears over this intensity gap were the primary motivation for the 2013 resignation of the then-61-year-old Keenan.[56]

An inescapable fact emerges from these statistics. While the percentage of Americans who are pro-life is steadily increasing, and a clear and substantial majority of Americans oppose the extremist abortion laws being passed in some states, these states, along with their liberal politicians and

Planned Parenthood, are foisting the very abortion procedures on the U.S. that more and more Americans are opposing. This is evidence of the arrogance and power Planned Parenthood, socialist/democrat politicians, academia, Hollywood, and the pro-death media have over America. They now publicly state that they will not stop until abortion during all nine months of pregnancy is available coast to coast for any reason.

Chapter 8–Arguments based on scientific evidence, and probing questions

Truth will always be truth, regardless of lack of understanding, disbelief or ignorance. – W. Clement Stone

W hy, in spite of all the evidence supporting life, are the anti-life forces becoming more entrenched in their delusional support for murder? One reason is that they must save face, even if it means putting themselves in the embarrassing position of denying truth. Since 1973 and before, they have gone down the road of advocating abortion over responsibility, and feel they can't or don't know how to turn back. For some, it is simply too much of a blow to their ego to have to admit they were wrong. For them, it almost seems preferable to continue to look foolish and disbelieve proven facts. For others, it may be blind allegiance to a political party that dictates what they believe, however heartless, wrong and disproven.

However, scientific facts and logic opposing abortion are overwhelming. If anti-lifers accept science and logic, their core beliefs have been dramatically challenged, and they would have to go back and reconsider who they are and what they believe in. It's much easier to reject it on its face. In that way, they don't have to confront their own beliefs. Some people would rather ignore evidence that contradicts their beliefs than be challenged.

There is another, more troubling explanation as to why anti-lifers so blindly refuse to give up their ideas and examine truth with an open and compassionate mind. The abortion debate has evolved into frightening new territory in the last ten years: anti-lifers are no longer able or willing to acknowledge the humanity of the unborn.

It is inexplicable that throughout history, people have convinced themselves that horrors such as slavery, the torture and killing of Jews, and now the killing of the unborn is justifiable. If you were a plantation owner in the antebellum south, you had to convince yourself that slaves were not human. If you were a Nazi in the late 1930's Germany, you had to convince yourself that Jews were not human. And if you are an anti-lifer today, you must convince yourself that the unborn are not human. When you disconnect yourself from the reality that the unborn fetus is a new, separate human being, and in this way dehumanize him, it becomes easier to justify killing him.

The proverbial "slippery slope" takes on hideous consequences in the context of the pro/anti life debate. Rarely do laws or social movements remain self-contained. They almost always expand and metastasize. In 1930's Germany, it became acceptable to boycott Jewish businesses. Then it became commonplace for authorities to harass Jews and close their businesses. Next, not much was said when Nazis began to remove Jews from their homes and restrict them to certain areas or ghettoes. After that, Jews started disappearing as they were dragged from their homes in the middle of the night. And finally came the brutal torture, starvation and medical experiments of the concentration camps.

Assisted suicide was first introduced in Europe, initially to allow those suffering from terminal diseases to end their lives.

Now, especially in the Netherlands and Belgium, the courts are filling up with cases of suspicious deaths, in which adult children convince their elderly parents they are a burden, and coerce them into killing themselves.[57] In 2019, a doctor in the Netherlands was trying to euthanize an elderly patient suffering from dementia, who had expressed a desire for assisted suicide "when the time was right." As her dementia progressed, the doctor determined it was time to end her life, even though the patient was not in agreement at the time. The doctor drugged the patient's coffee to sedate her, but the patient was still awake and struggling against the injection, so the doctor had the patient's family members hold the patient down while she killed her.[58]

In the example of abortion, in 47 short years we have gone from the legalization of abortion to legalized murder of babies hours away from birth, and wanting to allow babies born alive after unsuccessful abortions to die on the tables of abortion facilities.

These ideas always start out as "fringe" concepts with limited support. But if they are kept in the forefront of public awareness long enough, the initial shock starts to wear off and they start to seem more acceptable. Then comes legalization, and then comes expansion as we gain momentum sliding down the slippery slope. One of the latest "fringe" ideas that has appeared from two separate sources in the last five years is the idea of "post birth" abortion, whereby if your baby has become too inconvenient to care for after they're born, you can bring them into a "facility" where they will be given lethal injections and "put down" like an aging dog.[59-61] We are currently in the shock stage of this idea. Where will it end?

In any case, let's examine several arguments that anti-lifers use to justify abortion to themselves or others, and see why each one fails. These are responses the supporter for life can use to respond to arguments that abortion is acceptable.

"It's my body" This is one of the most overused and flawed arguments that pro-death proponents make. They claim that women, not the government, have the right to control their "own bodies". Very few would argue that the government or anyone else should have control over anyone's body. But if the human embryo and fetus are inconsequential "blobs of tissue" that are part of the mother's body, at what point do they become a separate human being?

The press and Hollywood would have us believe that the unborn child with its own unique DNA and beating heart are part of the mother and she should have the right to dispose of it as she has her hair cut or nails clipped. A person's hair and nails have the same DNA as the rest of his or her body. From the moment of fertilization, the new life does not have the same DNA as his mother. Anti-life proponents first try to cover up, and then become silent or offer a distracting argument at the scientific evidence that a unique person is created at conception. But human embryology textbooks have taught this basic fact for decades. Perhaps no one describes it more clearly than human embryologist C. Ward Kischer, Ph.D.:

> . . . in 1989 I came to the conclusion that the science of Human Embryology was being rewritten according to political correctness. . . Abortion, partial birth abortion, in-vitro fertilization, human fetal research, human embryo research, cloning and stem cell research are all core issues of Human Embryology. Yet, in all of the Supreme Court cases since 1973 and at all of the Congressional hearings on these issues, no human embryologist has been called as a

witness and no reference to Human Embryology has ever been made ... Justice Harry Blackmun wrote in the Roe v Wade decision: 'We need not resolve the difficult question of when life begins.' Blackmun smeared the distinction between the biological (or embryological) meaning with the legal meaning, and conflated the two into his declaration. His inference was that he was talking about biological life without specifically stating so.

From this source followed a science of Human Embryology that has been parsed and perverted, revised and redefined, changed and corrupted. ... The media have especially ignored Human Embryology in their many articles on the core issues. The media have preferentially published a distortion of this science while totally ignoring the many references available for factual information. The impact of this on public policy has been staggering. Every one of the core issues identified above is ultimately distilled down to the question of 'When Does Human Life Begin?'

The answer is there in the textbooks of Human Embryology, that 'human life' begins at fertilization, or conception, which is the same as fertilization. It has always been there, at least for 100 years. Yet, this simple fact, without referencing Human Embryology, has been parsed and corrupted into questioning whether life even exists at that time ... Every human embryologist, worldwide, states that the life of the new individual human being begins at fertilization (conception). Yet never does one see in the media, nor in the Councils identified above, such a reference, even though it is there in virtually every textbook. Every Human Embryology textbook, and every human embryologist, not only identifies the continuum of human life, but describes it in detail, which is to say:

At any point in time, during the continuum of life, there exists a whole, integrated human being! This is because over time from the one-celled embryo to a 100-year-old senior, all of the characteristics of life change, albeit at different rates at different times: size, form, content, function, appearance, etc.. [62]

Ronan O'Rahilly is the human embryologist who developed the classic Carnegie stages of human embryological development. He also sits on the international board of Nomina Embryologica (which determines the correct terminology to be used in human embryology textbooks). He states that

the fusion of the sperm (with 23 chromosomes) and the oocyte (with 23 chromosomes) at fertilization results in a live human being, a single-cell human zygote, with 46 chromosomes – the number of chromosomes characteristic of an individual member of the human species, not a blob of cells that are part of the mother's body.[63]

In the article "When do human beings begin?" published by Dianne Irving, M.A., Ph.D., from the American Bioethics

Advisory Commission, she states: "The question as to when a human being begins is strictly a scientific question, and should be answered by human embryologists." She thoroughly defines the necessary scientific terms, facts and concepts regarding the beginning of human life. She finds that

> scientifically, something very dramatic occurs between the processes of gametogenesis and fertilization – the change from two simple PARTS of a human being, i.e. a sperm and an oocyte (usually referred to as an 'ovum' or 'egg'), which simply possess 'human life', into a new, genetically unique, newly existing, individual, live human BEING, an embryonic single-cell human zygote. That is, parts of a human being have actually been transformed into something very different from what they were before; they have been changed into a single, whole human being. During this process, the sperm and oocyte cease to exist, and a new human being is produced.

Irving goes on to state . . .

> a human being is the immediate product of fertilization. As such he/she is a single-cell embryonic zygote, an organism with 46 chromosomes . . . This human being immediately produces specifically human proteins and enzymes, directs his/her own further growth and development as human, and is a new, genetically unique, newly existing, live human individual.

Irving dispels several common myths with scientific fact:

Given these basic facts of human embryology, it is easier to recognize the many scientifically inaccurate claims that have been advanced in the discussions about abortion, human embryo research, cloning, stem cell research, the formation of chimeras, and the use of abortifacients–and why these discussions obfuscate the objective scientific facts.

MYTH: (Anti life proponents say) 'Pro-life advocates claim that the abortion of a human embryo or a human fetus is wrong because it destroys human life. But human sperms and human ova are human life too. So pro-lifers would also have to say that the destruction of human sperms and human ova are abortions too–and that is ridiculous.'

FACT: As pointed out above in the background section, there is quite a difference, scientifically, between parts of a human being that only possess 'human life' and a human embryo or human fetus that is an actual 'human being.' Abortion is the destruction of a human being. Destroying a human sperm or a human oocyte would not constitute abortion, since neither are human beings. The issue is not when does human LIFE begin, but rather when does the life of every human BEING begin. A human kidney or liver, a human skin cell, a sperm or an oocyte all possess human LIFE, but they are not human BEINGS–they are only parts of a human being. If a single sperm or a single oocyte were implanted into a woman's uterus, they would simply rot. They would not grow as human embryos or human fetuses who are human beings.

MYTH: The product of fertilization is simply a 'blob', a 'bunch of cells', a 'piece of the mother's tissues.'

FACT: As demonstrated above, the human embryonic organism formed at fertilization is a whole human being, and therefore it is not just a 'blob' or a 'bunch of cells.' This new human individual also has a mixture of both the mother's and the father's chromosomes, and therefore it is not just a 'piece of the mother's tissues.' Quoting Carlson:

... [T]hrough the mingling of maternal and paternal chromosomes, the zygote is a genetically unique product of chromosomal reassortment, which is important for the viability of any species.

MYTH: The immediate product of fertilization is just a 'potential' or a 'possible' human being–not a real existing human being.

FACT: As demonstrated above, scientifically there is absolutely no question whatsoever that the immediate product of fertilization is a newly existing human being. A human zygote is a human being. It is NOT a 'potential' or a 'possible' human being.

MYTH: A single-cell human zygote, or embryo, or fetus are not human beings, because they do not look like human beings.

FACT: As all human embryologists know, a single-cell human zygote, or a more developed human embryo, or human fetus is a human being – and that that's the way they are supposed to look at those particular periods of development.

MYTH: The 'morning-after pill', RU-486, and the IUD are not abortifacient; are only methods of contraception.

FACT: The 'morning-after pill,' RU-486, and the IUD can be abortifacient, if fertilization has taken place. Then they would act to prevent the implantation of an already existing human embryo–the blastocyst – which is an existing human being. If the developing human blastocyst is prevented from implanting into the uterus, then obviously the embryo dies. In effect, these chemical and mechanical methods of contraception have become methods of abortion as well.

Ideas do have concrete consequences–not only in one's personal life, but also in the formulation of public policy. And once a definition is accepted in one public policy, the logical extensions of it can then be applied, sometimes invalidly, in many other policies, even if they are not dealing with the same exact issue–as happens frequently in bioethics. Thus, the definitions of 'human being' and of 'person' which have been concretized in the abortion debates have been transferred to several other areas, e.g., human embryo research, cloning, stem cell research, the formation of chimeras, the use of abortifacients–even the issues of brain death, brain birth, organ transplantation, the removal of food and hydration, and research with the mentally ill or the disabled. But both private choices and public policies should incorporate sound and accurate science whenever possible. What I have tried to indicate is that in these current discussions, individual choices and public policies have been based on 'scientific myth,' rather than on objective scientific facts.[64]

Professor Micheline Matthews-Roth from Harvard Medical School corroborates Dr. Irving's assessment: "It is scientifically correct to say that an individual human life begins at conception."[65] Even some in the abortion industry acknowledge this. Abortionist William Harrison states "No one, neither the patient receiving an abortion, nor the person doing the abortion, is ever, at any time, unaware that they are ending a life."[66]

The field of fetal surgery exists based on the medical fact that surgeries performed on pre-born babies to correct conditions and defects have high success rates. It recognizes that the fetus, a human being separate from the mother, is being treated. These surgeries have included shunting to bypass an obstructed urinary tract, removal of tumors at the base of the tailbone, and treatment of congenital heart disease. In June, 2019, the Cleveland Clinic performed one of the first successful surgical repairs of spina bifida on a preborn infant. Fetal surgery includes the separate provision of anesthesia to the baby.[67]

Clearly, in light of the previously mentioned research, the bodies of the unborn are not part of the bodies of the women carrying them, but a new, unique individual life. The anti-life proponents' argument that the unborn are part of the mother's body is so nonsensical they should be embarrassed to try to make that claim, yet they continue to flaunt their ignorance. After all, if the unborn child were part of his or her mother's body, pregnant women would have two heads, four arms, and four legs of their own, and give birth to parts of their own bodies. "Congratulations Mrs. Smith! You're the proud mother of your own foot!" is something that's never been heard in any delivery room.

What about cases of rape? Anti-life proponents believe that abortion is always a legitimate option for babies conceived by rape, and claim that the number of pregnancies begun by rape is substantial. The statistics prove otherwise. In studies published by Planned Parenthood's own Guttmacher Institute, they admit that less than 1% of all women seeking an abortion did so because of rape.[68]

But what we need to ask in the case of rape is "Who is the guilty party?" Why are we punishing with death the innocent life that was created in a rape instead of the rapist? The death penalty is not applied to rapists. Why is it applied to the innocent child? Rape is a horrific act of violence. Do we fix a horrific act of violence with another horrific act of violence? Is the life of a baby conceived in rape worth any less than one who is not? Ask this question of any of the thousands of Americans living productive, contented lives who were conceived in rape. Ask the same of their spouses, children, and grandchildren.

In 1990, a 19 year-old college student in Pittsburgh was pulled into an alley one night after leaving work and raped at knifepoint. A few months later she discovered she was pregnant as a result of the attack. She decided to allow her child to live and give him or her up for adoption. Her parents persuaded her to keep her child and they would help raise her. When the baby girl was born, she was given the name Valerie. Valerie grew up in a warm, loving home with her mother and grandparents. Fast forward to 2014 where a beautiful young woman, Valerie Gatto, was crowned Miss Pennsylvania and went on to represent her state at the Miss U.S.A. pageant. Today, Valerie's mission is to educate women on how to avoid sexual assault. Did Valerie deserve to be killed in utero? Does her life have any less value than yours or mine?

If the rape victim cannot bear to see her child who was conceived as a result of rape, why can't she give him or her up for adoption? According to American Adoptions, there are about 2 million couples currently waiting to adopt a newborn in the U.S., which means there are approximately 36 couples waiting for every child who is placed for adoption.[69]

What about pregnancies that threaten the life of the mother? Again, Planned Parenthood and other abortionists would have us believe that pregnancy is a "disease" to be "cured" by abortion, and often threatens the life of the mother. Again, medical research statistics prove this is not true. The Center for Disease Control shows that for 2014, the chance of a woman dying for reasons related to her pregnancy were .018%, and the great majority of these deaths happened in women who had no prenatal care. This .018% translates to less than two fatalities per 10,000 pregnancies, or approximately 700 deaths per year in the United States, according to the Center for Disease

Control. These deaths are evenly divided among three main causes: heart disease and stroke, obstetric emergencies during delivery, and post birth complications such as cardiomyopathy. Since most of these deaths occur unexpectedly either during delivery or after birth, it makes no sense to claim that one could predict those complications and have a pre-planned abortion that could save the life of the mother.

The CDC Director, Dr. Robert T. Redfield, who co-authored the research report states, "Ensuring quality care for mothers throughout their pregnancies and postpartum should be among our nation's highest priorities." CDC physician Wanda Barfield concurs: "Our new analysis underscores the need for access to high quality services, risk awareness, and early diagnosis, but it also highlights opportunities for preventing future pregnancy-related deaths." In no part of the study is abortion ever mentioned.[70]

Between six and nine percent of the maternal deaths are due to ectopic pregnancies, when the fertilized zygote implants somewhere outside the uterus, usually the fallopian tube. In this case, surgery is the recommended treatment. Once the surgeon locates the implanted zygote, it is removed. The zygote or embryo in an ectopic pregnancy cannot survive to full term, and if left unattended, puts the mother's life in danger. In this case, we save the life we can save, meaning the mother's life. This is different from an abortion. In an abortion, the intention of the procedure is to kill the fetus. In ectopic surgery, the embryo dies as an indirect result of surgery to save the mother's life, not directly from murder.

Especially after the point of viability, which currently is approximately 22-24 weeks gestation, there is never a reason to abort a baby due to complications for the mother. The baby is viable, you simply induce labor and deliver a healthy baby. At this point, the pregnancy has ended, and any pregnancy induced complications have no reason to continue. As of February, 2019, the Dublin Declaration on Maternal Healthcare had been signed by over 1,000 physicians, mostly obstetricians/gynecologists, and states:

> As experienced practitioners and researchers in obstetrics and gynaecology, we affirm that direct abortion – the purposeful destruction of the unborn child – is not medically necessary to save the life of a woman. We uphold that there is a fundamental difference between abortion, and necessary medical treatments that are carried out to save the life of the mother, even if such treatment results in the loss of life of her unborn child. We confirm that the prohibition of abortion does not affect, in any way, the availability of optimal care to pregnant women.[71]

Anti-life proponents also claim that restricting abortion causes a rise in maternal deaths. This is again, contrary to published facts. According to Rob Schwarzwalder and Cathy Cleaver Ruse, of the Family Research Council:

> Despite its tight abortion restrictions, Ireland has the lowest maternal mortality rate in the world (before the legalization of abortion), according to a study by several agencies at the United Nations. Malta also has substantial abortion limitations and yet has among the lowest maternal death rate world-wide, lower than the United States. Data compiled by Polish government agencies shows a marked decrease in maternal deaths once abortion was made illegal.[72]

With modern medical advances in the 21st century, the number of women dying for pregnancy-related reasons is approaching the nonexistent level. According to the Society for Maternal-Fetal Medicine, there are currently over 1,600 certified physicians in the United States working in the highly specialized field of high-risk pregnancy.

The reason anti-lifers greatly exaggerate the very rare instances of pregnancy due to rape and pregnancies that endanger the life of the mother is, of course, to encourage and justify all abortions. However, laws and public policy shouldn't be made based on a tiny number of outlying cases, but rather on the majority.

Planned Parenthood and other abortionists vigorously oppose abortion restrictions that include no exception for rape or health of the mother. However, when presented with an abortion law that does include these exceptions, they just as vigorously oppose it. Their main concern isn't really for the mother's safety. Their obvious goal is to enshrine abortion as a legal "right" during any phase of pregnancy and for any reason across the United States, and profit from it.

It's legal. True, and slavery was also legal in the United States for 246 years. In the Dred Scott case of 1857, the Supreme Court ruled that slaves were not U.S. citizens. In 1896, the Plessy vs. Ferguson Supreme Court ruling upheld the constitutionality of racial segregation laws for public facilities. Until 1920, it was legal to deny women the right to vote in the United States. In the 1944 case Korematsu vs. the United States, justices upheld the evacuation order against Japanese Americans to prison camps after the bombing of Pearl Harbor. Tom Best, acting dean of the Pepperdine Law School stated in 2011 that

> These cases show that the Supreme Court does make mistakes, that the justices aren't infallible

. . . They show that the justices will be subject
to the same interests and pressures of society
at the time they make decisions as any other
American.[73]

Obviously, just because something is legal, doesn't mean it's
morally correct.

**If abortion is outlawed, thousands of women will die
at the hands of back alley butchers doing illegal abortions,
as happened before Roe v. Wade.** Pro-death advocates like to
paint the image of widespread "back alley abortion" horror stories, conducted in grimy conditions by "butchers" before abortion was legal. Again, this is not accurate. In 1960, 13 years
before abortion was legalized, Dr. Mary Calderone, a former
medical director for Planned Parenthood, estimated that 9 out
of 10 illegal abortions were done by licensed doctors in their
offices: "they are physicians, trained as such..."[74]

In addition, the "yearly thousands" of women dying in
back alley abortions is also seriously suspect. As reported by
Schwarzwalder and Ruse:

. . . it is a fact that abortion industry insider
Bernard Nathanson admitted to circulating
false numbers. Dr. Nathanson co-founded
NARAL (originally called the National Alliance
to Repeal Abortion Laws and today, NARAL Pro-
Choice America) and was director of the Center
for Reproductive and Sexual Health in New York
City, at one time the largest abortion clinic in the
western world. In 1979 Nathanson said:

How many deaths were we talking about when
abortion was illegal? In NARAL we generally

emphasized the drama of the individual case, not the mass statistics, but when we spoke of the latter it was always '5,000-10,000 deaths a year.' I confess that I knew the figures were totally false, and I suppose that others did too if they stopped to think of it. But in the 'morality' of our revolution it was a useful figure, widely accepted, so why go out of our way to correct it with honest statistics? The overriding concern was to get the laws eliminated, and anything within reason that had to be done was permissible.[75]

Carole Novielli, of Live Action, revealed the results of her research on annual deaths of women due to illegal abortions before Roe v. Wade, in an article published on March 9, 2019. With sources that included Planned Parenthood's Guttmacher Institute, Planned Parenthood's former medical director, Dr. Mary Calderone, the Department of Health, Education and Welfare, Dr. Christopher Tietze, the Center for Disease Control, and Planned Parenthood itself, Novielli found that from 1950-1972, an average of 222 women died each year from illegal abortions, not the many thousands that anti-life proponents claim.[76] The murder of one innocent individual is unacceptable. But even with 222 deaths a year, the question now becomes: Which is the lesser evil, 222 lives lost a year, or the 850,000 lives lost to abortion each year in the United States?

Is it acceptable to legalize something just because some people will do it anyway? There will always be car thieves. Should we legalize car theft? Should we legalize sex trafficking because someone is always going to do it and by legalizing it, regulate it and make it safer?

It's a matter of conscience that should be left up to each woman. People who use this reasoning feel that abortion should be left up to each woman's individual conscience and no one else should be concerned. They often say, "I don't like abortion, I don't support abortion, but let's not prohibit it, let's leave it for each individual to decide for herself." What happens when we apply this reasoning to other serious issues? One argument would go something along these lines: "I don't like slavery, I'd never own slaves, but let's not outlaw it. Let's leave it for each individual to decide for himself." Or "I don't like child sex trafficking, I'd never participate in it, but let's not outlaw it, let's leave it up to each individual to decide for himself."

Advocates for this argument might say, "Well, slavery and child sex trafficking are not controversial, and in both of those cases, a person's rights are being violated, and physical and emotional harm and abuse are inherent parts of those trage-dies." Yes, slavery and child sex trafficking are two of the most horrific, inhumane, human rights abuses in our world and should never be permitted. But how tragic that the dismemberment and decapitation of innocent, defenseless human lives is not controversial for so many in our country. In addition, in an abortion, the act of being ripped limb from torso is the ultimate in physical harm, and the unborn child is denied the first and most basic human right, the right to life.

Why aren't you concerned about the homeless? What about all the children living in poverty?

Those anti-lifers who are awake enough to realize they have no logical, intelligent reasons left to defend preborn genocide but still refuse to rethink their position, lash out with responses that are more and more ineffective or even nonsensical. This "attach and distract argument" has become more and more common in the last few years as science has become more definitive in its proof of human life in the unborn.

First, if a person is caring enough to defend the life of the unborn, they are almost surely also going to be concerned with children and people at the margins of society. What the anti-life political left is trying to do is obfuscate and distract attention from an issue they can't win on logic and fact, so they attach issues to it that are almost universally agreed upon as compassionate. For the first 40 years since Roe v. Wade was passed, this "argument" didn't exist. These other issues are very important and need our attention as a country. However, they have never been, and are not part of the pro-life debate. Ben Shapiro cites this example:

> There's a (homeless) guy walking down the street. Should he be murdered or not? No. You're not taking him into your house, are you? I don't have to take him into my house to not want him murdered. They're two different issues. I don't have to adopt him, I just don't want to see him killed. Opposing murder doesn't mean it's your job to support the person.

One of the hypocrisies of the left is to point a moralistic finger at the pro-life community and virtue signal to insinuate that they are unconcerned with anyone in need, and couldn't care less about children born into difficult circumstances. Some of the things shouted at pro-lifers at prayer vigils besides obscenities and vulgarities are, "Are you going to take care of all those unwanted children?" and "How many children have you adopted?" They then drive off before they have to hear any response.

According to liberal New York Times journalist Nicholas Kristof, conservatives give more money to charity, including orphanages, than liberals.[77] Kristof's statements are backed up empirically by Arthur Brooks' book, "Who Really Cares?"[78]

It is very interesting to note that the same people who advocate for the lives of the homeless and immigrants (and rightfully so) are some of the same people advocating for ending the lives of the unborn. How does this work? How do we get to decide which lives are worth working to save and which we work to kill? (obviously an illegitimate question, as no one should be working to kill any human life.)

You pro-lifers are only concerned with babies before they're born. You're just "pro-birth". You're not interested in helping women in crisis pregnancies. Katie Franklin at Pregnancy Help News has the same information as other survey results: there are approximately 2,750 pro-life crisis pregnancy centers in the United States. These centers provide medical care, counseling, adoption referrals, parenting classes, maternity clothes, baby items, job counseling, emergency and long-term housing, legal support and much more to women in crisis pregnancies. Unfortunately, these centers are under continuous legal attack from Planned Parenthood and other abortion groups.[37]

Pro-lifers, conservatives and the religious right just want to take away women's rights and healthcare. Are there really groups out there today that want to take away women's rights? . . . to go back before 1920 when women didn't have the right to vote? And which rights are we talking about? The right to "choose"? Anti-lifers never seem to finish that sentence. The right to "choose" what? The right to choose to kill an innocent, defenseless, unborn human life if it's going to be too inconvenient to care for? The "right" to kill someone like that isn't a right. No one has the right to kill another innocent human being.

Is there really someone out there who wants to take away women's healthcare as Planned Parenthood makes it sound? Really? To put signs in doctors' offices all around the country stating "Men Only–No Healthcare For Women". This idea is ludicrous.

The problem is the way "healthcare" is defined. Contrary to what pro-death supporters would have us believe, abortion is **not** healthcare. *Health care*, by its very definition, is something that *cares* for someone's *health*. Stitching up a head wound is health care. Removing a cancerous skin lesion is health care. Physical therapy is health care. Decapitating and dismembering an unborn human being is not health care. It doesn't make the mother healthier and it certainly doesn't care for the health of the unborn child. It doesn't care for anyone's health, it's killing someone.

In her December 11, 2018 article in the National Review entitled "Health Care Doesn't Kill", Alexandra Desanctis summed it up better than anyone:

> Refashioning the meaning of words to fit political purposes is in vogue. This is perhaps nowhere more apparent than when proponents of 'the right to choose' insist that 'women's autonomy' is protected by the 'constitutional right to privacy' because of the 'intimate nature of personal health-care decisions.'
>
> They are speaking, inevitably, about abortion. But they rarely, if ever, can bring themselves to say the word. That's why Leana Wen–the new president of Planned Parenthood, with her singularly unconvincing veneer of naivete–has taken the helm and launched the institution's 'new vision,' summed up by the slogan 'This Is Health Care.' But it isn't, of course. You know that, and I know that, and Wen knows that. And that's

why she has to lie. No one, after all, wishes to be a loud public champion for the right to end the life of an unborn human being, which is, indisputably, what abortion does. That's an easy right to take issue with. It is much more difficult to explain why the government should be able to interfere with women's private medical decisions or, better yet, stand between them and the health care they need.

With this formula, Planned Parenthood has found a political winner. 'Health care' provides a very useful front for the hundreds of thousands of abortions that the organization performs each year–321,384, as of the group's last annual accounting. And that's why Wen, taking the reins from Cecile Richards, who led the group for more than a decade, is soldiering on with the former chief's sanitized version. This is health care. Hand over our half a billion dollars and move right along. Nothing to see here. Millions of women rely on Planned Parenthood for routine services, these smiling executives insist in every interview, never forced to confront the reality that federally qualified clinics across the country outnumber their own facilities 20 to 1.

If they must speak the word 'abortion', they assure us that this faceless procedure is only 3 percent of the group's work. And, after all, why shouldn't it be available? It's only *health care*. But even in our Orwellian age of reupholstering language for the sake of preserving the privilege of tossing away the unwanted unborn, we all know that health care doesn't kill. Sometimes technology fails us, and very often the sick die, in spite of the best efforts of doctors and progress. (But) as any doctor will tell you, true medicine never aims to end a life.

This is health care, they say. But health care for whom? A recent *Think Progress* interview with Wen informed readers that Planned Parenthood's new strategy is 'deceptively simple.' For perhaps the first time, *Think Progress* hits the nail on the head. Wen and her whitewashing warriors have rebranded killing as health care because no one–not even these zealous defenders of reproductive rights – wants to openly cheer for death. But what kind of monster, they wonder, wouldn't want women to have access to health care?So now abortion is health care, and Planned Parenthood's social–media gurus hammer home the message with frequent tweets repeating the refrain, as if by sheer incantation we may be brainwashed into agreeing.

It's a canny strategy, and so far, it seems to be working. The trouble for Planned Parenthood is that reality isn't on their side, and science can be kept at bay for only so long. Human beings have long debated the morality of early abortions and litigated the difference between late-term abortion and infanticide. Reasonable people can disagree over the ethics at stake in the competing rights of maternal bodily autonomy and the filial

right to life. Only a person with a deadened conscience can truly believe that the abortion debate
is a matter of *health care.* Setting a broken bone
is health care. Prescribing allergy medication is
health care. Performing open-heart surgery is
health care. Lethally injecting a living, entirely
unique human being and suctioning it from its
mother's womb piece by piece is not health care.
To say otherwise is total delusion or utmost evil.

There's a reason why defenders of abortion
rights refuse to define their terms. If they call
abortion what it is, they will lose. Many people
will speak up for women's autonomy. Many more
will defend the right to access health care. No
one wants to justify killing unborn human beings.
Not even Planned Parenthood will do that.[7]

Some of the arguments made by anti-lifers are so ridiculous,
it's surprising that they're not embarrassed to make them. For
example, it has been said that pro-lifers are in favor of legally
prosecuting women who have had abortions. Actually, they are
referring to proposed restrictions on abortions in which the
doctors who performed illegal abortions would be exposing
themselves to legal prosecution, not the women who had the
abortion. The desperate attempt at spin reached the point of
lunacy in early 2019, after Alabama and other states passed
laws protecting the unborn. Pro-death proponents were
spreading the unbelievable rumor that the new laws provided
for prosecution and jail time for women who had suffered a
spontaneous miscarriage. What was going to come next? Five
to ten years in the penitentiary for heart attacks? Ten years to
life for having a stroke? As Clark Forsythe, J.D. explains in an

exhaustive article for Americans United for Life entitled "Why the States Did Not Prosecute Women for Abortion Before Roe v. Wade", the notion of jailing women for having an abortion has never existed in the United States.[79]

I'm not ready for a baby right now. This is not the right time. I couldn't care for a baby. It would put a cramp in my lifestyle or career. I believe every child should be "wanted".

The medical elephant in the room that no one is mentioning of course, is the medical discovery made centuries ago, that sexual intercourse can lead to pregnancy, and if a man and women feel they're not ready for a baby, they should not have sexual intercourse. It's really not that difficult a concept to internalize, although the sexual and social revolution of the 1960's has done an excellent job of separating that fact from reality.

If you are not ready to take on the responsibility of owning, maintaining, and paying for a car, don't go to the car dealership. If you are not ready to go to college, or if this is not the right time, don't fill out that application. If you're not ready for a baby right now, or it's not the right time, but you bypassed the common sense described above and are now pregnant, or have made someone pregnant, is it acceptable to kill an innocent human being for your oversight? Fifty years ago, the answer generally was no. After the sexual revolution of the '60s stripped us of our moral conscience, the answer often is "yes."

The "cramp my lifestyle or career" argument for killing someone is even more disturbing. Is there any greater disdain for human life than killing someone for your own convenience? A common argument in this same vein is "We (I) can't afford to have a baby." But many women and girls in this position who decide to keep their child turn to family or other resources for help. There are several financial safety net programs such as

Women, Infants, and Children (WIC) Food and Nutrition Service, SNAP (food stamps), TANF (Temporary Assistance for Needy Families), etc. MSW Online lists 99 great organizations confronting poverty and hunger. A google search gives hundreds more organizations that help the needy. Many don't research the options for help, and easily convince themselves that they can't afford a child. It would be interesting to know if there has ever been, in the U.S., a woman and the baby she chose to have, who have died of starvation because she didn't have the money to feed herself or her child.

The tests came back and there's something "wrong" with the baby. (S)He wouldn't live anyway. First, if a baby would not live long after birth, what is the need for carrying out a murder? What is the problem with letting nature take its course and allow the infant to have a peaceful death in the arms of his parents instead of tearing him limb from torso and decapitating him in utero? Bishop Kevin Vann, of the Diocese of Orange in California tells the story of a couple whose unborn daughter Rylei was diagnosed before birth with severe handicaps.

> Given the choice to abort, the parents, Krysta and Derek, decided instead that their daughter Rylei should be born and that her organs would be donated upon her natural death. She lived for only a few days. But she transformed the lives of her parents – who are forever changed by knowing her – and the lives of all the infants who received her donated organs, not to mention their families, friends and so on.

> These infants will go on to have lives like the rest of us, full of dreams and joys among the disappointments and sadness. Such is the human

experience.. But all of this is made possible because of the life of this one child who only lived for a few days outside her mother's womb.[80]

Carrying a child that has a non-life threatening intellectual or physical challenge is one of the saddest situations a couple can face. Legalized abortion handed these couples a gut-wrenching decision: Do we allow our baby to live or not? Many people would not know how to wrestle with the despair of such a dramatic life and death decision. In the United States, 67% of parents faced with a diagnoses of Downs Syndrome decide to abort their child.[81]

But what about the misdiagnosis of prenatal mental and physical conditions? There are no hard statistics on the misdiagnosis rate of prenatal conditions, but there are many cases of women who decide not to abort their child based on a positive test result and have a healthy baby with no problems or challenges. Many couples who opt for abortion in these situations suffer and struggle with their decision for years afterward.

"What about babies who are not wanted, who would be born into suffering and neglectful and abusive families?"

Is it acceptable to kill someone if we *think* they will be born into poverty or will have a miserable childhood? If so, Oprah Winfrey would not exist today. Neither would J.K. Rowling, Abraham Lincoln, Benjamin Franklin, Walt Disney, or countless others who overcame adversity to become productive, contributing members of society. It's like saying to the unborn child, "we think you'll be born into poverty or abused or deserted by your parents, so we'll save you from that hardship and kill you before you even have a chance to overcome your obstacles. We wouldn't want to see anyone born into a less than perfect life, because it's not possible to rise above your circumstances."

It's so cruel to make a teenager carry a baby to term.

Which is more cruel, carrying a child till birth and then giving him up for adoption, or dismembering and decapitating that child in utero? What is so horrible about letting this child live and giving him up for adoption?

Men should have no say in abortion

What they really mean is pro-life men should have no say in abortion, as this argument is used only against pro-life men. If a man is anti-life, his opinion always counts. In fact, in an attempt to rally as many people as possible to support abortion, and therefore, their bottom line, years ago Planned Parenthood created the "bro-choice" campaign, and welcomed anti-life men into the fold. Abortion advocates welcome those irresponsible, abusive, misogynistic men dragging their wives or girlfriends to an abortion clinic against her will.

Anti-lifers often complain that they don't want a group of men deciding what they "can and can't do with their bodies", but they forget it was 9 men who legalized abortion. They also forget that most abortionists are men.

Should stay-at-home moms who aren't earning a salary have any say on tax policies?

During the civil war, the south's "states' rights" argument was that since the north didn't have slaves, people in the north should have no input regarding slavery.

The flawed argument that often follows is that it is "unfair" that women must bear the responsibility of carrying and giving birth to babies. In today's context of worshipping at the altar of comfort and convenience, and avoiding social and personal responsibility, this self-centered and immature attitude might seem completely logical. However, wisdom tells us that life is often not fair. Is it fair that children are abducted, tortured and murdered? Is it fair that we must watch cancer, Alzheimer's and other life-threatening diseases steal our loved ones?

To juxtapose the "unfairness" of women "having to" bear children versus men not having the same "burden", is it fair that women live, on the average, 5.1 years longer, according to U.S. census data?[82] Is it fair that almost 48,000 more men will be diagnosed with cancer than women this year, according to the American Cancer Society?[83] Is it fair that almost four times as many males as females die by suicide, according to the Centers for Disease Control and Prevention?[84] If it weren't for men, there wouldn't be a need for abortion. Does the father have no say in what happens to his child? Today, there are groups to support men who have missed out on fatherhood because their child was aborted and they had no voice in trying to save him/her. Are men not allowed to save lives, especially ones they have helped create? And isn't it a sexist philosophy to say a gender isn't allowed to have an opinion on a topic?

Whatever the pro-life or anti-life argument may be, it is necessary to delve to the core of a controversy to have the ability to identify and ask the appropriate questions; questions that will cut to the heart of the discussion, laying bare the central idea of the issue and facilitating logical thought and reasoning and the search for supporting evidence.

To that end, there are a few precise and powerful questions to be asked here if the preceding arguments are still ineffective in making the argument for life to an anti-lifer:

First, is the woman who enters an abortion clinic carrying something living or nonliving? i.e. something alive, or an inanimate object such as a doorknob? The obvious answer is "living".

Second, is she carrying a life separate from her own? In light of scientific research by human embryologists, the obvious answer is "yes."

Third, is this a human life? Here, the answer is even more obvious, or do women become pregnant with aardvarks and kangaroos? Do two human adults create a human fetus? Connecting the obvious answers to these questions leads to the conclusion *that this is human life, separate from the mother.*

Fourth, does abortion end this human life? Pro-life groups call abortion "murder", but what exactly is murder? What does it mean "to kill?" In deconstructing these definitions, it could be argued that to kill someone means to intentionally inflict sufficient physical damage so as to stop their heart from beating. The American Pregnancy Association as well as the National Institute of Health state that by 3 weeks after fertilization, the preborn child's heart is already beating.[85] So by the time a woman knows she is pregnant, the fetal heart is already beating. If we accept from Irving's research that from the moment of conception, a new person is created, and the physical violence of an abortion stops his heart from beating, then isn't abortion the murder a human being? Even in the event that an abortifacient is used in a chemical abortion before the formation of a human heart, during the first few weeks after fertilization, that human life, with its own unique DNA, dies.

On February 14, 2019, Kentucky Educational Television posted a video on YouTube of the discussion of SB 9, brought by Senator Matt Castlen, Republican from western Kentucky. Testifying in favor of this bill protecting the unborn after testimony against it was Abby Johnson:

> . . . one thing that I kept hearing is that there are no exceptions in this bill for rape, incest, etc. Let me be clear, even if there were, the ACLU wouldn't support it. Even if there were, Planned Parenthood wouldn't support this bill. So the fact

that they're even bringing that up, is really intellectually dishonest....

I want to talk specifically about what a first trimester abortion is, and what it looks like from a person who ran a Planned Parenthood abortion facility and was there for eight years. . . a transvaginal ultrasound is standard procedure inside of every national abortion federal clinic, which includes every Planned Parenthood clinic. That transvaginal ultrasound is done primarily for one reason: to determine how far along the woman is in her pregnancy, so that we know how much to charge her for the abortion. After the ultrasound is performed, the ultrasound machine is rolled away. The doctor comes in, who by the way has no conversation with the woman before the abortion. The fact that many people say abortion should be a decision made between a woman and her doctor is laughable. There is never a time where the abortion doctor goes in, sits down with the woman, and goes over risks, alternatives, and benefits to abortion. It does not happen.

The doctor starts performing the abortion . . . he's going to insert that suction probe inside of the woman's uterus. Ultrasound guidance is not used. That is not the standard protocol inside of National Abortion Federation or Planned Parenthood clinics. He's going to take that probe and he's going to blindly poke around inside the woman's uterus, until he thinks he has enough blood and tissue in a glass jar. That glass jar is going to go into a lab, called the POC lab. POC in the medical community stands for 'products of conception.' The products of conception are of course the baby. But you can't say baby inside the abortion clinic, so we said POC or if the staff was feeling funny, they would say that it stood for 'parts of children.'

After all the parts were accounted for, the POC lab technician would dump everything out into a glass baking dish that sat on top of an x-ray light box, and she would reassemble the parts of the baby. Please understand me, I am talking about first trimester abortion. Yes, there are parts. Yes, they must be reassembled. The baby is fully formed, every internal organ is formed by 12 weeks gestation. So yes, there are parts, even earlier than 12 weeks.

Once all the parts are reassembled, that POC tech will take everything, dump it into a red bio-hazard ziplock sort of bag, and those bags will go into a freezer in the POC lab, that the staff jokingly called 'the nursery.' And once a week, a company, a biohazard medical waste company like Stericycle will come into the facility and they will pick up all the red bags of babies where they are taken to their facility to be incinerated. That's if the abortion facility decides they don't want to just put them in their industrial size garbage disposer and grind them up and put them into the water waste treatment facilities.

That is first trimester abortion. . . . science also tells us that from the moment of conception, a unique, individual and unrepeatable DNA is formed. That DNA is human. Never in the history of the world has a woman delivered a cat or a dog, or any other species other than human. That's science. Our history tells us time and time again, that it is unjust to take the life of an innocent human being. It was unjust to dehumanize an entire segment of people when we were working to abolish slavery. It was unjust to dehumanize an entire group of Jewish people in the holocaust. But those two examples that I just gave you only exist because our society was willing to turn a blind eye, look a human person in the face, and say 'that is not a human being.' That is not scientific.

Now we are living in such depravity that there are people, like the people that oppose this bill, that are willing to say, 'I know it's a human being. I know it has a heartbeat, I know there is life there, and I know it is innocent, and I'm willing to kill it.' We have sunk to a new low in our society, and it is time for us to rectify what we have done.

So if you are a person here who has had an abortion, (turns and gestures to Nicole Stipp, who gave testimony in favor of abortion and proudly tried to justify her own abortion) I encourage you to seek healing, because abortion is not normal. Taking the life of an innocent human being that

is your own flesh and blood . . . is not normal.
And there are healing resources available. And
to the people in here who work in the abortion
industry, I encourage you to seek healing from a
ministry called 'And Then There Were None.' We
can get you out of the industry, and we can get
you into a line of work that you can actually be
proud of. And to the ACLU, (turns, gestures, and
looks at the ACLU Advocacy Director of Kentucky,
who in her testimony said 'this bill is patently
unconstitutional, the second it is signed, we will
bring a lawsuit') I can say affirmatively, we look
forward to your lawsuit.[86]

The law passed with the unanimous vote of all the committee members. The main point to be made here is that there
is never an excuse for killing an innocent, unborn human life.

Yet, it is inexplicable that there are those who claim to
believe abortion is wrong, yet believe it should be legal on the
grounds that "I don't think government should tell people what
they can and cannot do." People with this belief overlook the
fact that government dictates that its citizens leave their home
or place of employment, sometimes against their will, to serve
jury duty. Government has used the military draft to forcibly
send people to war. There are innumerable laws dictating that
all citizens pay income taxes, property taxes, buy auto insurance, wear motorcycle helmets, etc. As unpopular as these prac-
tices may be, the great majority of people comply. They had no
problem with government intervening to allow the unborn to
be killed, yet how is it that they don't believe that government
should step in to prevent millions of unborn lives being lost?

There are also many who claim that they don't feel abortion is right, but are "pro-choice." What kind of twisted logic is

this? The word "choice" means having alternative options available at one's disposal. How is it possible to endorse having two options, but not support one of them?

In 2004 NASA scientists landed two robotic rovers, Spirit and Opportunity, on Mars. One research interest was the possibility "that it (Mars) may once have harbored primitive, bacteria-like 'life'." How is it that bacteria on Mars is considered "life," yet many pro-death advocates refuse to recognize that a pregnant woman is carrying human life? Is there any more flawed and hypocritical situation than an abortion advocate spouting off about reproductive "rights" and then asking that person if they are glad their mother didn't abort them? What is so wrong about giving these unborn children life? What is so horrible in letting them live and allowing them to be adopted by a loving family who wants them?

Dr. Anthony Levatino observes that NARAL Pro-Choice America posted this message on its Facebook page: "We're part of the 7 in 10 who support Roe v. Wade because we believe everyone should decide for themselves whether, when and with whom to have a family." His response: Yes, agreed, everyone should make those decisions for themselves, but they should be made in a humane, intelligent way: choosing not to become pregnant in the first place, instead of acting irresponsibly and then killing the preborn as a way of 'deciding for themselves whether, when and with whom to have a family.'

Chapter 9–The Ten Universal Principles and more legal issues (philosophical, ethical and legal proof)

Morality is the basis of things and truth is the substance of all morality.- Mahatma Gandhi

O ne of the most compelling arguments for respecting and protecting human life is embedded in one of the most important philosophical works of our time. Father Robert Spitzer, SJ, who holds three master's degrees and a PhD, is a Jesuit priest, world renowned scholar, author, philosopher, educator, speaker and former president of Gonzaga University. He received the Bunn Medal for Most Outstanding Faculty Member at Georgetown University, and the award for outstanding faculty member in the College of Arts and Sciences at Seattle University. He has written numerous articles on leadership, metaphysics, ethics, and ontology of physics. He is the author of at least five books, among them *The Spirit of Leadership: Optimizing Creativity and Change in Organizations,* and *Healing the Culture: A commonsense Philosophy of Happiness, Freedom and the Life Issues.* He is the founder and president of the Spitzer Center of Ethical Leadership, which helps corporations and non-profit organizations develop leadership, constructive cultures, and virtue ethics. He is also the founder and president of the Magis Center of Reason and Faith, a non-profit organization dedicated to producing books, articles, documentaries, videos, and new media materials on the relationship between physics, philosophy, reason, cosmology, metaphysics, astrophysics and faith. He founded and is active in the leadership of Colleagues in Jesuit Business Education located in Seattle, Washington, University Faculty for Life in Washington, D.C., and co-founded Healing the Culture, a Seattle-based organization dedicated to developing educational materials on the philosophical under-pinnings of life issues, particularly "beginning of life" and "end of life" issues and how they affect and are affected by the notions of "happiness, virtue, freedom, love, personhood, suffering and the common good." He also founded Philosophical Foundations of Physics at Georgetown University. In addition, he is the co-director of the Institute on Faith and Reason at Gonzaga University, which, according to their website,

> is dedicated to developing an integrationist understanding of faith and reason through a philosophical investigation into both the nature and results of scientific research and through critical discussion and reflection on topics in philosophical theology.[87]

In addition to these, he is a member of at least seven boards of directors and trustees of various organizations. Fr. Spitzer has also produced seven television series for EWTN and gives approximately 60 public speeches per year. He appeared as a panelist, along with Stephen Hawking and Deepak Chopra, on a *Larry King Live* full-hour prime-time feature dealing with the relationship of faith and reason.

But perhaps Fr. Spitzer's greatest work is a book entitled "Ten Universal Principles: A Brief Philosophy of the Life Issues." In describing his work, he explains

> What becomes legal becomes normal, and because it is legally sanctioned, what becomes normal becomes moral. And that is a problem. Legal sanction leads to normality. Normality leads to some sort of moral sanction — everybody is doing it. So what we have is a general cultural problem. So I took the 10 principles that ground any healthy civilization and I said: Here is what civilization rests on and has always rested on. People know that if you give up objective truth then we are left with the strongest will or influential will, or whoever can get the most money mustered for a campaign wins. Might makes right. Anytime you have these 10 principles undermined, you have very deep cultural problems.[88]

The Catholic Education Resource Center states that the principles "form the foundation of civility, justice, and objectivity in cultures throughout the world."[89] Leslie Malek at WordPress. com sums up how vital these principles are to our civilization.

> How do we figure out what's right and what's wrong in politics — and in life? A slim book by Rev. Robert J. Spitzer, J.S., Ph.D, *Ten Universal Principles: A Brief Philosophy of the Life Issues*, drives ten stakes in the ground that firmly anchor any discussion about values in the face of moral relativism.

Father Spitzer explains the ten principles that go to the heart of what reasonable people believe about the dignity of life in all societies. The presence of these principles 'assures the possibility of humane civilization and their absence opens the path for corruption, deceit, injustice, and cultural decline,' explains the author. These ten principles are based on reason, ethics, justice, natural rights, identity, and culture and undergird every society that thrives. The discussion of each principle has a direct application to life choices that every woman and man faces, at home, at work, at play, and in the voting booth. . . . The discussions are linked to the U.S. Constitution, the U.S. legal, natural law, and the Magisterium of the Catholic Church.

Last but not least, the discussions give examples of how progressives and especially the abortion industry purposefully pervert these principles in order to justify their agenda — the culture of death and moral relativism. . . . We need to understand not only the playbook of this 'progressive' agenda but also the objective reasoning that explains why that playbook is twisted and corrupt. Harassment of the Church by the media and governments at all levels is a perfect example of the perversion of the principles. . .

Discussions based on emotion open a wide door to the justification of moral relativism. Examples of typical relativistic justifications of abortion include this kind of thinking: 'This is my body. I can do what I want,' 'Her child would be a burden,' 'We prefer to wait. We don't feel ready for a child,' or 'He doesn't want a child.' We ... need to recognize why the abortion industry's appeals to passion, prejudice, and pseudo-science are absurd and deceptive. We need to marshal the power of logic and objective reasoning to expose the absurdity and deceit of these arguments used by the people around us, the media, elected representatives, and government officials.

Well-told truth is far more attractive and enduring because it brings people to life. *Ten Universal Principles: A Brief Philosophy of the Life Issues* gives us 10 time-tested tools that help us firmly anchor our day-to-day defense of the sanctity of life in well-told truths.[90]

When confronted with anything that smacks of even the slightest spiritual argument, most atheistic anti-life proponents dismiss it immediately as right-wing evangelical extremist propaganda, and are not open minded enough to consider it. However, many of Fr. Spitzer's principles are rooted in secular and ancient Greek philosophy and obvious common sense. Fr. Spitzer himself said that his book "is not starting from a religious grounding. ... if you use the principles, they can't relegate you to a corner. These principles are what is holding the center together."

The principles are organized into four groups: The Principles of Reason, The Principles of Ethics, The Principles of Justice and Natural Rights, and The Fundamental Principle of Identity and Culture.

I. Principles of Reason (evidence and objective truth)

1) The Principle of Complete Explanation (from Socrates, Plato, and Aristotle) The best opinion or theory is the one that explains the most data.

2) The Principle of Noncontradiction (Plato and Aristotle) Valid opinions or theories have no internal contradictions.

3) The Principle of Objective Evidence (Plato and Aristotle) No arbitrary opinions or theories are based upon publicly verifiable evidence.

II. Principles of Ethics

4) The Principle of Nonmaleficence (Jesus, Moses, and worldwide religious traditions) Avoid unnecessary harms; if a harm is unavoidable, minimize it.

5) The Principle of Consistent Ends and Means (Saint Augustine) The end does not justify the means.

6) The Principle of Full Human Potential (Las Casas) Every human being (or group of human beings) deserves to be valued according to the full level of human development, not according to the level of development currently achieved.

III. Principles of Justice and Natural Rights (political justice and the dignity and treatment of human beings within civil society)

7) The Principle of Natural Rights (Suarez, Locke, Jefferson, and Paine) All human beings possess in themselves (by virtue of their existence alone) the inalienable rights of life, liberty, and property ownership; no government gives these rights, and no government can take them away.

8) The Principle of the Fundamentality of Rights (Suarez, Locke, and Jefferson) The more fundamental right is the one which is necessary for the possibility of the other; where there is conflict, we should resolve in favor of the more fundamental right.

9) The Principle of the Limits to Freedom (Locke and Montesquieu) One person's (or group's) freedoms cannot impose undue burdens upon other persons (or groups).

IV. Fundamental Principle of Identity and Culture

10) The Principle of Beneficence (Jesus) Aims at optimal contribution to others and society. *The Golden Rule: Do unto others as you would have them do unto you.*[91]

These rights and principles are so basic and profound that Fr. Spitzer states that "the evolution of culture and civilization has arisen" out of their development. He further contends that

> Failure to teach and practice any one of these principles can lead to an underestimation of human dignity, a decline in culture, the abuse of individuals and even groups of individuals, and an underestimation of ourselves and our potential in life.

> Failure to teach and practice several of these principles will most certainly lead to widespread abuse and a general decline in culture.[91]

Ethics is a fundamental part of Spitzer's ten principles. He defines "ethics" as being "concerned with

> ... the pursuit of what is good and avoidance of what is evil or harmful. It is a much older pursuit than the study of reason and natural rights, because it seems to have been integral to human consciousness at its origin. As philosophers, theologians, legal theorists, and political theorists reflected on the grounds and legitimacy of law and the legal system, they noticed one particular ethical ground that seems to be universally present in every culture and religion, a ground without which all law and legal systems lose their intelligibility and legitimacy – namely, the principal of non maleficence (avoiding unnecessary harm to others, Principle 4). .... this great principle not only stands at the foundation of

ethics and law, but also at the foundation of justice and rights. If this principle falls within a culture, then it is inevitable that the rest of ethics, justice, rights and law will fall along with it... we cannot live long without it.[91]

The Principle of Non maleficence is also known as "The Silver Rule" (as compared to "The Golden Rule"): Do not do unto others what you would not have them do unto you. There are also two important corollaries of the Principle of Non maleficence: the principle of consistency of ends and means (Principle 5) and the principle of full human potential (Principle 6). Spitzer emphasizes their importance because "without these three ethical principles, we may as well not proceed to the principles of justice and natural rights, for they would be unintelligible and without foundation." Principle 3 (The Principle of Objective Evidence, first proposed by Plato and Aristotle) explains that non arbitrary opinions or theories are based upon publicly verifiable evidence.

An example of objective evidence cited in Spitzer's book is that of Dr. Jerome Lejeune, the world renown French geneticist who discovered the link of disease to chromosomal abnormalities, and specifically his discovery that Down syndrome was caused by an extra copy of chromosome 21. Spitzer further explains that

> A DNA sequencer was constructed in the late 1980s, which enabled Dr. Jerome Lejeune and others to be certain of the presence of a unique full human genome in a single-celled human zygote. As was noted above, a full human genome in a zygote (the initial cell formed when a new organism is produced by sexual reproduction)

> constitutes a distinct and unique human being
> whose identity and DNA is not reducible to the
> mother's.[91]

Verifiable evidence such as Dr. Lejeune's work takes center stage in the abortion debate. The Ten Universal Principles demonstrate how deeply flawed some U.S. Supreme Court decisions were, how they should have been informed by ethics and verifiable evidence, and the enormity of their tragic consequences.

As Americans, we assume to a certain extent that our government has created an infrastructure of public protection to assure that the creation, interpretation and enforcement of laws, at least as it was envisioned by the founding fathers, would ensure justice and domestic tranquility for the common good. It is unsettling at best and frightful at worst, therefore, to realize that the U.S. Supreme Court, which is entrusted with the welfare of the legality of our society, has made some horrific mistakes. One example is their ruling in the 1857 Dred Scott case in which they declared that slaves are not citizens as defined in the Constitution

> and can therefore claim none of the rights and
> privileges which that instrument provides for
> and secures to citizens of the United States. On
> the contrary, they were at that time considered
> as a subordinate and inferior class of beings, who
> had been subjugated by the dominant race, and
> ... had no rights or privileges but such as those
> who held the power and the Government might
> choose to grant them.[92]

Spitzer points out "three violations of two of the ten universal principles" in the *Dred Scott* case. The first was that the Court "chose not to judge this 'class of beings' according to their full potential, but rather on the basis that their 'ancestors were imported into this country, and sold as slaves'", which violates Principle 4, that of non maleficence. He also points out that "the justices were either unaware of natural rights or simply assumed that people of African descent did not have natural rights" (because they were considered subordinate and inferior).[91] In either case, the Principle of Non maleficence was violated again.

In addition, Spitzer notes the third violation of the ten universal principles. . .

> the justices assumed that all rights are derived from the Constitution and that constitutional rights belong only to 'citizens'. Notice that the justices believed that they had the authority to declare who had the right to life, liberty, and property ownership by declaring who was a citizen. Since they seem to have been unaware of the existence of natural rights, and believed themselves to be bound only to the defense of constitutionally declared rights, the power to declare citizenship became the power to declare who had a fundamental right to liberty. Thus, the justices believed they had the power to declare that certain human beings did not have a right to liberty.[91]

Pro-death proponents will scoff at this example from 160 years ago as totally irrelevant to the current day and will fail to see the similarities in the *Roe vs. Wade* decision 116 years later.

However, the parallels are striking. In examining the majority's reasons more closely, Spitzer highlights . . .

> the uncanny resemblance between the *Roe v. Wade* decision and the *Dread Scott* decision with respect to the forgetfulness (or perhaps culpable neglect) of *natural* rights. In this case, the majority fixed its attention solely upon discovering the *constitutional* rights of the fetus. Recall that natural rights are the ground and purpose of all governmental authority (including the courts'), which makes the *first* purpose of every court the protection of natural rights. This, in turn, legitimizes its authority to interpret statutory law and adjudicate disputes.[91]

The following are three important parts of the *Roe vs. Wade* decision:

> 1. That since "no (previous legal) case could be cited that holds that a fetus is a person within the meaning of the Fourteenth Amendment . . . persuades us that the word 'person' as used in the Fourteenth Amendment, does not include the unborn."
>
> 2. "We need not resolve the difficult question of when life begins."
>
> 3. "When those trained in the respective disciplines of medicine, philosophy, and theology are unable to arrive at any consensus, the judiciary, at this point in the development of man's

knowledge, is not in a position to speculate as to the answer."[93]

However, the majority of the justices evidently felt that they *were* in a position to allow the unborn to be killed, even when they admitted that doubt existed as to when life begins.

Fr. Spitzer demonstrates that

> This reasoning of the majority is logically fallacious (violating Principles 1-3), completely ignores the natural rights of prenatal human beings (violating Principle 7), does not assess human life according to its full potential (violating Principle 6), and, as a consequence, sanctions a serious violation of the principle of non maleficence (Principle 4, the bedrock of all ethics). In short, it abrogates just about every principle of humaneness and civility and cannot be considered anything better than a disaster in the history of civilization.[91]

In agreement with Thomas Jefferson and John Locke, Spitzer states that

> Votes and statutory prescriptions are not infallible. What makes them legitimate is their operation within the contours of the natural rights of all persons. Thus, a majority cannot vote out the natural rights of a minority, for such a vote would be illegitimate because it negates the ground and purpose of the governmental authority through which the vote originated.

When the majority (of the justices) narrowed the criterion for the protection of unborn life to whether such life was protected under the Constitution alone, it abdicated its first duty to protect natural rights. In so doing, it undermined its own authority, which delegitimized its ruling. The majority might insist that it has the authority, but inasmuch as its actions undermine its own authority, such insistence is empty.

The idea of a natural right is to preserve life, not to kill it, and a constitutional right cannot supersede the natural right to life. The whole point of natural rights is that they cannot be superseded by the power of the state.

At this juncture, the majority shifted its burden of proof to a much easier bar to reach. Instead of justifying why a human life would *not* be considered a person, which is a burden of proof that the majority must meet in order to prevent a violation of the principles of natural rights and non maleficence, it shifted its burden to justifying why a human life *should* be considered a person. Obviously, this is an easier burden of proof to meet because one does not have to assume from the beginning that all human beings are persons. ... the Court would not have to show why human beings born in other countries should *not* be considered persons; it would only have to show why those foreign human beings. . . *should* be considered persons. Is there a use of the word 'person' in the Constitution that specifically applies to foreign human beings? Uh-oh.

According to this logic, the Court could sanction any penalty for any particular group of human beings simply because the Constitution did not explicitly mention them as 'persons'. Notice how this same reasoning is used in the *Dred Scott* decision, where the Court did not believe that it had a burden to prove why black human beings should *not* be considered citizens, but only why black human beings *should* be considered citizens. When it could find no such proof in the Constitution, it allowed them to be enslaved. The fallacious and harmful logic of the *Dred Scott* and *Roe v. Wade* decisions are identical. . . . the majority searched the Constitution . . . .to find any use of 'person' and when it found the Constitution silent on this topic, it interpreted that silence to mean that the Constitution did *not* intend to include the unborn . . . this reasoning goes against the centuries-old dictum, which has been embraced by American jurists from the beginning of this country, that silence has little probative value, because it literally provides no evidence in the affirmative or the negative.[91]

Spitzer summarizes by stating that in other words, if the Constitution mentioned "unborn life", then its intention was "to include unborn life within the scope of 'persons deserving protection under the law'". However, after changing their burden of proof to why unborn life *should* be considered persons, and finding no mention of "unborn life" in the Constitution, (silence), they assumed "that the Constitution did not intend to include unborn life within the scope of persons deserving protection under the law."

Spitzer poses and answers a key question as to why the majority of the justices in both the *Dred Scott* and *Roe v. Wade* cases "violated a centuries-old prohibition of construing silence to be valid evidence."

> It seems that they did not want to stop at anything preventing them from reaching their pre-determined conclusions. They wanted these conclusions so much that they were willing not only to jeopardize millions of human beings and risk the undermining of all prescriptive laws in the legal system, but also to risk centuries of criticism when their reasoning was exposed as fallacious and in violation of their own rules of evidence.[91]

After Dr. Lejeune proved scientifically that from the moment of conception, a single-celled zygote has a full human genome and constitutes a distinct and unique human being whose identity and DNA is separate and different from its mother, Fr. Spitzer noted that. . .

> he later testified to this fact in 1991 in *New Jersey v. Alexander Loce* and in 1992 in *Davis v. Davis*. This showed that the Supreme Court was unjustified in rushing toward its decision, which resulted in a violation of the principle of non maleficence, and that, if it were truly uncertain about whether a human being was present in the womb, it should have deferred

any decision about abortion until new technologies could make a clear scientific determination about the presence of human life. The Court did not revisit the criteria used in the *Roe v. Wade* decision, which makes it at least as unjust as the *Dred Scott* decision. Recall that a majority's justification by uncertainty has a fundamental flaw because uncertainty proves nothing objectively. It only manifests subjective ignorance. It is not the presence of evidence, it is the absence of the knowledge of evidence.

The 'reasoning' of the majority of the Court in *Roe v. Wade* was grounded in a gratuitous and destructive assumption: when in doubt, *assume* that human life does not exist, and *assume*, as a consequence, that the killing of such life can be sanctioned. Attend to the majority's reasoning here:

. . . . 'We need not resolve the difficult question of when life begins.' When those trained in the respective disciplines of medicine, philosophy, and theology are unable to arrive at any consensus, the judiciary, at this point in the development of man's knowledge, is not in a position to speculate as to the answer.

The obvious problem here is the majority's willingness to sanction killing through abortion when it was (by its own admission) *uncertain* about the presence of human life. If the judiciary did not believe that it was in a position to determine when human life begins, it should never have touched a case (let alone issued a decision) in which it might claim (let alone would claim) that human life was *not* present, which, if this claim is mistaken, would therefore sanction that life being killed. The principle of non maleficence requires that if one is not certain about the presence of human life, one must refrain from actions that could end a human life in the event that one is present. If one is uncertain about whether a being of human origin is really human, then one should presume that it is human because it came from human beings. To do otherwise is not only irresponsible (because one could illegitimately sanction killing out of uncertainty), but also unreasonable (because one should not expect anything other than human life to come from the reproduction of human beings).

The majority claimed that it consulted with many scientific, philosophical, and theological authorities, yet concluded in the absence of a consensus that the killing of human life is legally permissible. It never left open the possibility that new future technologies would be able more precisely to determine whether human life was present. Instead of deferring a decision about the case until such new technologies could resolve the question more clearly, it rushed toward a decision that amounts to a violation of the principle of non maleficence.

As mentioned above, the majority enshrined this 'irrational rationale' in a Supreme Court precedent. The highest court in the land declared that in the case of pregnancy when there is doubt about the presence of human life, it is justifiable to abort the fetus even though one may be killing a human being.

This absence of certainty has been used throughout history to attempt to justify bias, marginalization, segregation, oppression, and even genocide. Even the greatest skeptic about 'slippery slope' arguments should feel some trepidation about doing this.[91]

Fr. Spitzer clearly describes how the pro-death legal system twisted the definitions of "person" and "human being" to fit the convenience of their ruling in *Roe v. Wade*:

As can be seen from the above, the majority's attempted justification of its actions turns on its definition of 'person'. Let us examine its 'reasoning' here:

If this suggestion of personhood is established, the appellant's case, of course, collapses, for the fetus' right to life would then be guaranteed specifically by the Amendment. The appellant conceded as much on reargument. On the other hand, the appellee conceded on reargument that no case could be cited that holds that a fetus is a person within the meaning of the Fourteenth Amendment. (Section IX.A)

The majority (and even the appellant seeking legal abortion), by their own admission, realized that if personhood could be established, then the appellant's case in favor of abortion would collapse. As will be shown below (Principle 7), this reasoning is backward. The Court did not have to *establish* the existence of personhood in a being of human origin with a full human genome. It should have *presumed* personhood in order to prevent a gross violation of the principle of non-maleficence. This principle requires that the Court *establish* that personhood does not exist if it wants to sanction the killing of beings of human origin with a full human genome.

... 'personhood' is not merely a *legal* concept; it is essentially an *ontological* concept (i.e., it defines what a being is, namely, human) and an *ethical* concept (i.e., it defines the kind of being that we are obligated not to kill, abuse, or harm unnecessarily because of its intrinsic worth as human). The majority's claim that the absence of a case is sufficient to establish the non-presence of personhood in a fetus, therefore, is a gigantic error of omission (Principle 1). It hasn't even begun to establish the nonpresence of personhood on either an ontological or an ethical level.

If the majority had made recourse to the linguistic history of 'person' (and had, thereby, become acquainted with the ontological meaning of 'person', a human being) before seeking a legal definition of it from case precedents, it would not have separated 'person' from 'human being' and would have presumed that the human fetus is a person because human fetuses are genetically distinct human organisms, rather than parts of human organisms. If the Court had waited for ten years, it would have found sufficient technological verification of this presumption through the DNA sequencer. Therefore, the majority would have had to have concluded on the basis of (1) linguistic usage and history, (2) common sense (human fetuses come from human beings), and (3) scientific evidence (the presence of a full human genome in a zygote; see above), that the human fetus is indisputably a person.

Instead of making recourse to the ontological definition of 'person', the majority decided to restrict itself to a legal definition. It then found itself (conveniently) in need of a case precedent to determine whether a human fetus was a person. When (not surprisingly) it could not find such a case precedent (because the personhood of human fetuses had not previously been taken up by the United States Supreme Court), they concluded that human fetuses were not persons!

In *Roe v. Wade*, the majority ignored these precedents and chose, rather, to argue a logical fallacy. This fallacy can be easily seen when one considers that every new definition of a term will never be found in a case precedent (old definitions) precisely because it is new. Trying to determine whether a human fetus is a person by means of U.S. Supreme Court case precedents when such cases had not previously arisen is like trying to establish the nonexistence of the North American continent prior to the time of Christopher Columbus by looking at maps made prior to his voyage, noticing the absence of any such continent, and concluding from its absence on these maps that it did not exist at that time. Thankfully, the scientific world did not have to suffer from this self-contradictory methodology.

Inasmuch as the majority failed to look at the linguistic history of 'person', failed to see the primary meaning of personhood as ontological (as a human being), failed to assume that human parents would conceive human beings, failed to await potential scientific confirmation of the humanity of the fetus, and failed to correct itself when indisputable scientific confirmation of a full human genome in a single-celled human zygote became known, could it have done anything on the *legal* front to avert its highly problematic declaration on personhood? They could have done as the court of Georgia did in *Tucker v. Howard Carmichael & Sons*, when it cited the *Blackstone Commentaries on the Laws of England*. Note that the *Blackstone Commentaries* makes recourse precisely to a common usage and ontological definition:

If the majority had followed the example of the *Blackstone Commentaries*, the Georgia court in *Tucker v. Howard Carmichael & Sons*, the New

Jersey Supreme Court in *Raleigh Fitkin-Paul Morgan Memorial Hospital v. Anderson*, the District of Columbia district court in *Simmons v. Howard University*, and the Nevada Supreme Court in *Weaks v. Mounter* in turning to a common and ontological definition of person-hood (instead of irrationally trying to find a legal definition from case precedents that had not yet considered the question), it would have come up with a very different definition of per-sonhood – one that did not break with either the common law or state supreme court prec-edent; one which did not introduce a spurious distinction between ontological personhood and legal personhood (based on a spurious distinc-tion between 'person' and 'human being'); one that did not rush into an egregious violation of the principle of non maleficence through the arbitrary use of that spurious distinction; one that was legally and ethically responsible. The majority would have decided that 'persons" are human beings, and that human fetuses are per-sons because they are human beings, which can be known by the fact that they are beings of human origin and can now be seen to have a full human genome irreducible to either one of his parents. It would have concluded in *Roe v. Wade* that the appellant's case collapsed, using its own reasoning that 'if this suggestion of personhood is established, the appellant's case, of course, col-lapses, for the fetus' right to life would then be guaranteed specifically by the Amendment.'

Once it is established that a particular being is a human being, then it is established that the being has ontological personhood. Once ontological personhood is established, then ethical personhood follows. Ethical personhood simply means applying the principle of non maleficence (the most fundamental standard of ethics) to an ontological person (that is, to a human being). When we recognize the ethical personhood of a human being, we must recognize its legal personhood, because the law cannot undermine its most fundamental ethical standard (the principle of non maleficence) without undermining itself.

The immensely troubling dimension of the majority's rationale in *Roe v. Wade* is that it has now set within U.S. Supreme Court precedent its spurious distinction between ontological and legal personhood and sanctioned its irrational attempt to justify the non presence of person-hood on the basis of case precedents that had not considered the question.

Legal personhood is not defined into existence by lawyers; it exists in the intrinsic worth of existing human beings. When one separates legal personhood from ontological personhood, abuses always follow because one has to be a certain kind of human life in order to qualify for protection under the law. But every qualification is a form of exclusion and marginalization of some minority . . . History is replete with examples of how this was done to Indians, black people, Jews,

Gypsies, and all the victims of euthanasia (based on diminished capacity). It has now been done again using the same logic in the *Roe v. Wade* decision.[91]

Fr. Spitzer reflects on the gravity of not correctly weighing the important issues in arriving at such a supremely crucial decision as protecting human life:

> The above long string of logical errors leading to the sanctioning of a gross violation of the principle of non maleficence must give us pause. Could intelligent people really have done this without some degree of awareness of (and culpability for) its problematic character? Didn't they even have a hunch that something might be seriously wrong? The only way of redressing this is to overturn the decision upon which it is based. This alone will restore the principle of non maleficence in our culture.
>
> At this point, you may have surmised that the uncompromisable nature of the principle of non maleficence is grounded in the presumption that human beings have very special inherent or intrinsic value – and in the minds of many philosophers, *transcendent* value. Thus, human beings cannot be treated like mere inanimate objects or even like nonhuman animals. There is something about human beings that merits uncompromisable special protection, which does not allow for exceptions.

This awareness is not restricted to religiously or spiritually inclined people, nor to philosophers such as Plato and Aristotle; it pervades the common sense of virtually every human being.

So why do philosophers, scientists, and people of common sense assert that human beings have such a special value? The answer lies in several interrelated observations. These observations are present in the works of many philosophers and scientists, beginning with Socrates, Plato, and Aristotle, moving through Saint Augustine, Maimonides, Averroes, Saint Thomas Aquinas, Francisco Suarez, John Locke, Immanuel Kant, G. W. F. Hegel, John Henry Newman, and into the twentieth and twenty-first centuries (e.g., Edmund Husserl, Edith Stein, Jacques Maritain, Henri Bergson, Emerich Coreth, Bernard Lonergan, and many others). This idea is also central to the works of many prominent physicists and biologists in the twentieth and twenty-first centuries. One example comes from the great physicist Sir Arthur Eddington, who observed, after detailing the equations of quantum physics and relativity physics:

We all know that there are regions of the human Spirit untrammeled by the world of physics. In the mystic sense of the creation around us, in the expression of art, in a yearning towards God, the soul grows upward and finds the fulfillment of something implanted in its nature. The sanction for this development is within us, a striving born

170

within our consciousness or an Inner Light proceeding from a greater power than ours. Science can scarcely question this sanction, for the pursuit of science springs from a striving which the mind is impelled to follow, a questioning that will not be suppressed. Whether in the intellectual pursuits of science or in the mystical pursuits of the spirit, the light beckons ahead and the purpose surging in our nature responds.[91]

In a Live Action article from June 1, 2017, Calvin Freiburger references an article in the Harvard Journal of Law and Public Policy written by Harvard law student Josh Craddock.

A truly originalist answer to the question of personhood has to consider what the word 'persons' was understood to mean when the Fourteenth Amendment was written and ratified.

He proceeds to explain that layman's dictionaries treated the concepts of humanity and personhood interchangeably, and so did legal terminology–more explicitly so, in fact . . . Craddock notes that Blackstone expressly recognized that personhood and the right to life existed before birth with a simple and clear legal standard: 'where life can be shown to exist, legal personhood exists.' . . .

Craddock shows that many of the states that voted to ratify the Fourteenth Amendment had also criminalized abortion, meaning they understood personhood then in much the same way that pro-lifers understand it now: By the time of the Fourteenth Amendment's adoption, 'nearly every state had criminal legislation proscribing abortion,' . . . Indeed, 'there can be no doubt whatsoever that the word 'person' referred to the fetus.' In twenty-three states and six territories, laws referred to the preborn individual as a 'child.' Is it reasonable to presume that these legislatures would have used this terminology if 'they had not considered the fetus to be a 'person?''

When the Amendment was adopted in 1868, the states widely recognized children in utero as persons. . . . Senator Jacob Howard, who sponsored the Amendment in the Senate, declared the Amendment's purpose to 'disable a state from depriving not merely a citizen of the United States, but any person, whoever he may be, of life, liberty and property without due process.' Even the lowest and 'most despised of the (human) race' were guaranteed equal protection. . .The primary framer of the Fourteenth Amendment, Representative John Bingham, intended it to ensure that 'no state in the Union should deny to any human being . . . the equal protection of the laws.'

The past four decades' worth of abortion jurisprudence has nothing to do with legal merit and almost everything to do with the partisan politics of the presidents who nominated judges and the senators who reviewed them. So while this rot has been allowed to fester for a long time,

there are no legal barriers keeping us from challenging it–we need only the will and imagination
to change our tactics.[94]

So what exactly did Roe v. Wade do? Some people assume
that the Court made abortion legal in the first trimester of
pregnancy only, and that it was subject to substantial limits
and regulations, neither of which is true. As summarized by
Schwarzwalder and Ruse,

> The Supreme Court in Roe v. Wade did not create
> a limited right to abortion but a virtually unlim-
> ited right to abortion throughout pregnancy.
>
> Here's how: The case involved an 1854 Texas law
> prohibiting abortion except 'for the purpose of
> saving the life of the mother.' The plaintiff, whose
> real name is Norma McCorvey, desired a purely
> elective abortion and filed suit claiming the
> Texas law deprived her of constitutional rights.
>
> Seven members of the Supreme Court agreed.
> While admitting that abortion is not in the text of
> the Constitution, they never the-less ruled that a
> right to abortion was part of an implied 'right to
> privacy' that the Court had fashioned in previous
> rulings regarding contraception regulations.
> ('Privacy' is not in the text of the Constitution
> either.) They also ruled that the word 'person' in
> the Constitution did not include a fetus.[8975]
>
> . . . The Court ruled that abortion must be per-
> mitted for any reason a woman chooses until

the child becomes viable; after viability, an abortion must still be permitted if an abortion doctor deems the abortion necessary to protect a woman's 'health,' defined by the Court in another ruling issued the same day as 'all factors—physical, emotional, psychological, familial, and the woman's age—relevant to the well-being of the patient.'

In this way the Court created a right to abort a child at any time, even past the point of viability, for 'emotional' reasons. Stated another way, the Supreme Court gave abortion doctors the power to override any abortion restriction merely by claiming that there are 'emotional' reasons for the abortion. Abortion advocates want to hide this, of course, but liberal journalists such as David Savage of the Los Angeles Times have reported the truth about Roe, saying the Supreme Court created an 'absolute right to abortion' under which 'any abortion can be justified.'[95]

Roe v. Wade was so flawed that a long and growing list of prominent "pro-choice" legal commentators now call Roe v. Wade indefensible. The late John Hart Ely of Yale, for instance, argued that Roe was wrong "because it is not constitutional law and gives almost no sense of an obligation to try to be."[96] The law clerk of Justice Blackmun, the Justice who authored the Roe v. Wade opinion, calls it "one of the most intellectually suspect constitutional decisions of the modern era."[97]

The Washington Post's legal editor said it has "a deep legitimacy problem."[98] Even Justice Ruth Bader Ginsburg has been critical of Roe, saying that it "ventured too far in the change it ordered and presented an incomplete justification for its action"[99] and that the Roe decision was "not the way courts generally work."[100]

Cal Thomas of the Chicago Tribune describes how Roe v. Wade was based on a fabrication from the very beginning:

> Legal abortion was conceived in a lie. Norma McCorvey, 'Jane Roe,' claimed to have been raped. She later admitted lying in order to make her case more compelling to the Supreme Court. The justices who made abortion legal believed testimony that thousands of women were dying from illegal abortions, a 'fact' asserted by the National Abortion Rights Action League, but later acknowledged to be false by top NARAL official Dr. Bernard Nathanson, who was at the time operating the nation's largest abortion clinic in New York.[101]

Norma McCorvey was the "Jane Roe" in the Roe vs. Wade case that legalized abortion in 1973. After the court ruling, she worked in abortion clinics before becoming pro-life in 1995. In a January, 2016 article in "Live Action News", Sarah Terzo reports on some interesting insights from McCorvey in "7 powerful quotes from Jane Roe of Roe v. Wade":

1. The entire basis for Roe v. Wade was built upon false assumptions.

2. I didn't know during the Roe v. Wade case that the life of a human being was terminated.

3. The courts ... I feel used me to justify legalization of terminating the lives of 35 million babies.

4. There were dead babies and baby parts stacked like cord wood. (Describing a typical clinic where she worked in 1995).

5. No one even explained to the mother that the child already existed and the life of a human was being terminated.

6. Clinic workers suffer, the women suffer, and the babies die.

7. I long for the day that justice will be done and the burden from all of these deaths will be removed from my shoulders.[102]

Chapter 10–Planned Parenthood, masters of deception

In a time of universal deceit, telling the truth is a revolutionary act.- unknown

T he United States has had a long history of corporate and business formation that has driven the largest economy in the world for many years. U.S. universities' schools of business are world renown. It is undeniable that the American entrepreneurial spirit is known throughout the world and throughout history as leading the nation-building efforts of the United States since the 18th century. Every major U.S. corporation has divisions and departments devoted to marketing, development and innovation that keep that company viable and ensure its existence and growth.

Planned Parenthood also works with vigorous zeal to expand its "services", although since they are in the business of death, must resort to deceiving the public to stay in business. To make matters worse, they use tax dollars to promote their business of death and deception, and to aggressively pressure and support politicians, who will, in turn, support them once in office.

How many of our tax dollars do they receive? According to statistics from Planned Parenthood's own yearly report, we paid $563,800,000 (the largest amount to date) to the country's leading abortionist organization in 2018.[103] The data from their 2018 balance sheet show an additional $365,700,000 from something called "Non-government health services revenue", and $104,800,000 in "Other operating revenue".[104]

But between 2012 and 2016, they donated $38,000,000 to political campaigns of anti-life politicians.[105] Where is the public outcry over this? There is none, because this news has been stifled by the anti-life media.

According to Planned Parenthood's consolidated financial statements, the business of death is very lucrative. For example, their financial statements show that their total assets increased by $249,000,000, and their total revenue by $205,000,000 in only one fiscal year, from 2017 to 2018. In fact, as can be seen in Figure 1 below, their total net assets have increased every year since at least 2009, and their total revenue has increased every year since 2015. Interestingly absent from their financial statements, however, is the amount of money earned from performing abortions.

Figure 1

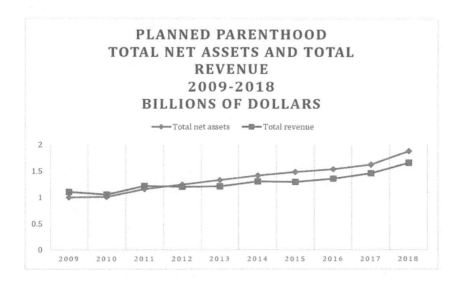

Adapted from Planned Parenthood annual reports, 2009-2018
https://www.scribd.com/document/49124420/Planned-Parenthood-Annual-Report-08-09 https://issuu.com/actionfund/docs/ppfa_financials_2010_122711_web_vf?viewMode=doublePage https://issuu.com/action-fund/docs/ppfa_ar_2011_110112_vf https://www.plannedparenthood.org/files/4913/9620/1413/PPFA_AR_2012_121812_vF.pdf https://www.plannedparenthood.org/files/7413/9620/1089/AR-FY13_111213_vF_rev3_ISSUU.pdf https://www.planned-parenthood.org/files/6714/1996/2641/2013- 2014_Annual_Report_FINAL_WEB_VERSION.pdf https://www.plannedparenthood.org/files/2114/5089/0863/2014-2015_PPFA_Annual_Report_.pdf https://www.plannedparenthood.org/uploads/filer_public/18/40/1840b04b-55d3-4c00-959d-11817023ffc8/20170526_annualreport_p02_singles.

pdf https://www.plannedparenthood.org/uploads/
filer_public/71/53/7153464c-8f5d-4a26-bead-2a0d-
fe2b32ec/20171229_ar16-17_p01_lowres.pdf https://www.
plannedparenthood.org/uploads/filer_public/80/d7/80d-
7d7c7-977c-4036-9c61-b3801741b441/190118-annualre-
port18-p01.pdf

To be sure, Planned Parenthood offers traditional, beneficial medical services such as STD testing and cancer screenings.
These services, along with glowing pictures of healthy, smiling,
laughing, celebratory young women in upscale surroundings
are touted front and center on their website, and also are used
to pump up the clean cut image Planned Parenthood uses to
disguise their darker side: abortion, which they have duped
the country and the world into thinking is part of "healthcare"
and "reproductive rights".

Dictionary.com defines "healthcare" as "the field concerned
with the maintenance or restoration of the health of the body or
mind."[106] Webster's New Collegiate Dictionary defines it as "the
prevention or treatment of illness by doctors, dentists, psychol-
ogists, etc.; efforts made to maintain or restore health especially
by trained and licensed professionals."[107] Webster's also defines
abortion as "a medical procedure used to end a pregnancy and
cause the death of the fetus."

The obvious question is: How could any rational, literate
person possibly define the "prevention or treatment of illness"
and "the maintenance or restoration of . . . health" as causing
"the death of the fetus?" Yet again, pro-death supporters want
us to believe that abortion is "healthcare."

However, the number of abortions they perform continues
to rise. In fact, since abortion became legal in 1973, the percentage of abortions performed by Planned Parenthood versus
total abortions performed in the United States has increased

every year except two.[110] In 2015, they performed 34.9 percent of all abortions in the United States, and that figure rose to 38 percent in 2017.[111] Figure 2 shows the number of abortions Planned Parenthood has performed in the past several years: [109]

Figure 2

Figure 2

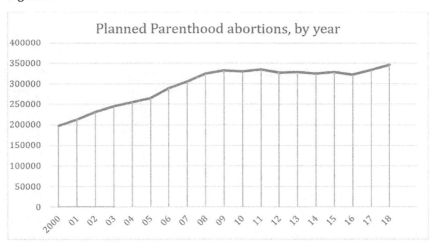

Adapted from ADF – Planned Parenthood by the numbers and Planned Parenthood annual reports, 2012-2018 http://www.adfmedia.org/files/ PlannedParenthoodNumbers.pdf https://www. plannedparenthood.org/files/4913/9620/1413/ PPFA_AR_2012_121812_vF.p df https://www. plannedparenthood.org/files/7413/9620/1089/ AR- FY13_111213_vF_rev3_ISSUU.pdf https://www. plannedparenthood.org/files/6714/1996/2641/2013- 2014_ Annual_Report_FINAL_WEB_VERSION.pdf https://www. plannedparenthood.org/files/2114/5089/0863/2014-2015_ PPFA_Annual_Report_.pdf https://www.plannedparenthood.

org/uploads/filer_public/18/40/1840b04b-55d3-4c00-959d-11817023ffc8/20170526_annualreport_p02_singles.pdf https://www.plannedparenthood.org/uploads/filer_public/71/53/7153464c-8f5d-4a26-bead-2a0d-fe2b32ec/20171229_ar16-17_p01_lowres.pdf https://www.plannedparenthood.org/uploads/filer_public/80/d7/80d-7d7c7-977c-4036-9c61-b3801741b441/190118-annualreport18-p01.pdf

However, Planned Parenthood has always been quick to downplay their role in abortion and try to boast of the legitimate healthcare services they offer. (Although in recent years they have begun to blatantly advertise that they are the leading provider of abortion in the U.S.) But data from their annual reports taken from their website demonstrates that they have become less and less about these healthcare services they hide behind, than their devotion to abortion. According to Planned Parenthood's own figures, they did 371,997 more cancer screenings in 2011 than the figure listed in their 2013-14 report, and conducted 4416 fewer STD tests during the same period. Prenatal services, which to begin with, are almost nonexistent at Planned Parenthood, dropped by almost half between 2014 and 2015.[105] In 2015, they did less than one percent of all Pap tests in the U.S., only 1.8 percent of all clinical breast exams, and no mammograms.

Another smokescreen perpetrated by Planned Parenthood is the ostentation that they provide a variety of options for the woman facing an unintended pregnancy, including adoption. However, in their 2012-13 Annual Report, they reveal they did only 2,197 adoption referrals. That number dropped to 1880 the next year, which amounts to one adoption for every 149 abortions, comparatively speaking.[108]

The following Figure 3 illustrates that although the rise in the number of abortions they perform continues to increase (albeit slightly), the number of other legitimate services they provide are in decline.

Figure 3

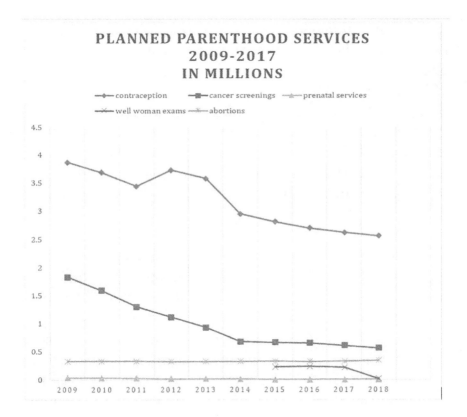

Adapted from Planned Parenthood annual reports 2009-2018

https://www.scribd.com/document/49124420/Planned-Parenthood-Annual-Report-08-09 https://issuu.com/actionfund/docs/ppfa_financials_2010_122711_web_vf?viewMode=doublePage https://issuu.com/

actionfund/docs/ppfa_ar_2011_110112_vf https://www.plannedparenthood.org/files/4913/9620/1413/PPFA_AR_2012_121812_vF.pdf https://www.plannedparenthood.org/files/7413/9620/1089/AR-FY13_111213_vF_rev3_ISSUU.pdf https://www.plannedparenthood.org/files/6714/1996/2641/2013-_2014_Annual_Report_FINAL_WEB_VERSION.pdf https://www.plannedparenthood.org/files/2114/5089/0863/2014-2015_PPFA_Annual_Report_.pdf https://www.plannedparenthood.org/uploads/filer_public/18/40/1840b04b-55d3-4c00-959d-11817023ffc8/20170526_annualreport_p02_singles.pdf https://www.plannedparenthood.org/uploads/filer_public/71/53/7153464c-8f5d-4a26-bead-2a0d-fe2b32ec/20171229_ar16-17_p01_lowres.pdf https://www.plannedparenthood.org/uploads/filer_public/80/d7/80d-7d7c7-977c-4036-9c61-b3801741b441/190118-annualreport18-p01.pdf

Obviously, as their beneficial services decline and the number of abortions they perform increase, Planned Parenthood is becoming more and more invested in the business of abortion, contrary to what they publicly state. However, they walk a fine line. As they claim abortions account for only 3% of their services, they also want pregnant girls and women to know that, according to their website, "abortions are a safe way to end a pregnancy" and that everyone's doing it. Their website has an entire section devoted to abortion, and claims that "abortions are very common. In fact, 3 out of 10 women in the U.S. have had an abortion by the time they are 45 years old." They admit that some states "may require one or both of your parents to give permission for your abortion or be told of your decision prior to the abortion. However, in most states you can ask a judge to excuse you from these requirements," and they are there to help girls circumvent these obstacles.[112]

The anecdotal accounts of what really happens when a young, unmarried, pregnant girl comes to a Planned Parenthood clinic seeking information and guidance are plentiful. Online research provides case after case in which girls are pressured to have an abortion quickly, often using high pressure sales tactics, such as one price for the abortion today, a higher price if they wait.

Martin Fox, of the National Pro-Life Alliance states that

> Abortionists routinely lie about abortion – to the public, to the media, and especially, to the women. Former abortion clinic workers have repeatedly spilled the beans about what really goes on in so-called 'counseling' sessions.

> The first and greatest lie all abortion workers are trained to propagate is the dehumanization of a woman's baby. Abortionists tell women that their unborn child is nothing more than a blob of tissue, even though nothing could be further from the truth. Never is the word 'baby' heard from an abortionist's lips, only 'cells, tissue, blob, and it.'

> But the lies don't stop there. Story after story has been written about the abortion giant Planned Parenthood claiming to offer women 'caring counsel' while in reality exerting cold-hearted pressure to abort. Abortion workers prey upon women's fears, even threatening price hikes for hesitant women in order to pressure them

> to abort. The coercion from abortionists even becomes physical. One former clinic worker tells of seeing a 17-year old girl dragged literally kicking and screaming by her aunt and 'counselor' into the abortion room.
>
> Another woman had a last minute change of heart and decided to choose life, but the abortion assistant held her down on the examination table while her baby was ripped from her.
>
> Far from promoting 'women's health,' abortion mills promote the death of unborn babies through the deception of their mothers.[113]

Planned Parenthood is not content with ending over a third of a million lives a year in the United States. They are also active in Africa and Latin America. Again, their website is full of statements of how their interest lies in helping underserved women in these countries obtain health care services, but also admit that these "health care services" include abortion. In countries that have a long history of valuing life, Planned Parenthood's website used to state that they "support efforts in developing countries to change the social, legal and political climate surrounding access to comprehensive reproductive health care including safe and legal abortion." (That statement has since been removed from Planned Parenthood documentation). Evidently Planned Parenthood feels it is their right to change the cultural, social, legal and political systems of other countries.

In her book "Target Africa–Ideological Neocolonialism in the Twenty-First Century", Obianuju Ekeocha describes how first world countries are pushing their agendas of "population control, hypersexualization of youth, radical feminism, (and) abortion . . ." onto African nations, and tying financial aid to the adoption of these left-wing ideologies.

She describes how pro-family traditions have been at the heart of African culture for millennia, and how the "developed" world is destroying African society by forcing their liberal agendas on her people. She claims that what results is a new ideological colonialism in the twenty-first century. This, in spite of a 2013 study she cites by the Pew Research Center that polled over 40,000 Africans in forty countries that shows that over 80% of Africans find abortion morally unacceptable.

To illustrate Planned Parenthood's arrogance in deciding every country in the world needs to dehumanize the unborn and subject them to a gruesome death, Ekeocha prints a full copy of an e-mail Laurie Rubiner, Planned Parenthood vice-president of Public Policy and Advocacy sent to then Secretary of State Hillary Clinton. In this e-mail Ms. Rubiner requests that Clinton pressure the Kenyan government to not include a fetal personhood amendment to its constitution. Ekeocha goes on to explain that

> When calling on favors and twisting arms do not work, our modern-day colonial masters resort to dragging African leadership into expensive legal battles. In 2015, when the Kenyan government decided to prohibit abortion training for healthcare workers, the director of medical services revoked the national abortion-training manual . . . In retaliation, the Center for Reproductive Rights (CRR), an organization founded in America and headquartered in New York, filed a lawsuit against the Kenyan attorney general, the Ministry of Health, and the director of medical services. Their African regional director accused

the Kenyan government of allowing thousands of women in Kenya to die or to suffer severe complications needlessly from 'unsafe' abortion: . . . Medical professionals in Kenya must be trained and given clear standards and guidelines on providing women who qualify for services and need to end a pregnancy with safe, legal care. . . . One cannot help but wonder how an American pro-abortion organization became an advocate for all Kenyan women of reproductive age. It seems a classic case of unsolicited interventionism enabled by paternalism.

Ekeocha also cites a publication from the International Planned Parenthood Foundation that is distributed in Africa entitled, *"Healthy, Happy and Hot"*. In the section regarding people infected with HIV, the booklet says that two types of people in the target audience are:

- Young people living with HIV who are married, in a relationship with one or more partners, as well as those who are single, dating, or just want to have sex.- Young people living with HIV who are just starting to think about dating and sex as well as those who have more experience.

She continues to cite from the part of this publication, describing how Planned Parenthood encourages young people with HIV to behave:

. . . first they stress that 'being in a relationship with someone who has HIV is just as fulfilling and satisfying as with anyone else.' One might not be able to compare his relationships, however, because the party with HIV is not obligated to disclose that he is infected with the virus: 'Some countries have laws that say people living with HIV must tell their sexual partner(s) about their status before having sex, even if they use condoms or only engage in sexual activity with a low risk of giving HIV to someone else. These laws violate the rights of people living with HIV by forcing them to disclose or face the possibility of criminal charges.'

The booklet goes on to encourage HIV-positive people to enjoy sex in whatever way they want, regardless of the consequences to anyone else: 'There is no right or wrong way to have sex. Just have fun, explore and be yourself!' It also encourages high-risk behavior: 'Some people have sex when they have been drinking alcohol or using drugs. This is your choice ... If you want to have sex and think you might get drunk or high, plan ahead by bringing condoms and lube or putting them close to where you usually have sex.'[8]

Planned Parenthood even tells us how to have a relationship, and automatically assume relationships must include sex. In a part of their website that has since been removed, entitled "How to Have a Great Relationship", sex is front and center, as if it were an automatic and necessary component of a beginning relationship. In fact, in the section entitled "Relationships" they never once referred to simply a romantic relationship, but always called it a "romantic and sexual relationship".

Currently, part of their website reads, "We've got the facts you need, from practicing safer sex to figuring out what turns you on." "Reading or watching porn" is listed as a "kind of sex that people have."

They urge parents of preschoolers to teach their children that "most girls have vulvas and most boys have penis/testicles" because "some people with gender identities 'boy' or 'man' have vulvas and some with the gender identity 'girl' or 'woman' have penis/testicles." They advise that when an elementary school aged child (5-8) asks about sex, a good explanation is

> If they ask what the word sex means, you can say
> something like: Sometimes when two grownups
> like each other, they want to kiss and touch
> each other's bodies — especially their penis or
> vulva. [114]

They obviously have no confidence that people can act as humans who are able to exercise self-control, or really need to, because their doors are always open to help people end a resultant human life that is too inconvenient.

Planned Parenthood and other abortion supporters also assume that everyone engages in risky sex; "risky sex" being people engaging in sex before they are ready; sex that puts them at risk for a pregnancy before they are able to handle the demands of a baby; sex that has caused the rate of STD's to soar in recent decades. Planned Parenthood assumes that we no longer have the ability to make positive choices for ourselves that are in the best interest of our own well-being, and when a pregnancy occurs, they are there to provide "health care."

As mentioned earlier, one of the most widely circulated claims Planned Parenthood makes is that only 3% of their services are abortion. These figures are highly manipulated, and a video by Live Action illustrates just how deceptive they are. According to their own annual report, Planned Parenthood does more than 300,000 abortions a year. Dividing the number of abortions they perform in a year by the number of patients they see a year shows that one in every eight women who go into a Planned Parenthood clinic will get an abortion. But to get their 3% figure, they divide the number of abortions by the number of "services" they provide, which they describe as a "discrete clinical interaction." They then count all their "services" equally, regardless of the cost, time, or effort it takes to render that service. Therefore, an entire abortion procedure, which can cost from $390 to $1,500 is counted the same as a pregnancy test, which can be bought at a pharmacy for $10.

In other words, Planned Parenthood maximizes the number of "services" by counting every single thing they do, no matter how small, as a separate "service". In this way, they are able to count 9.4 million "services". Dividing the 323,999 abortions they performed in 2014 by 9.4 million "services", they arrive at the 3% figure. For example, a girl goes into a Planned Parenthood clinic and gets her pregnancy test, the abortion procedure, an STI test, and some contraceptives. In one visit she gets four services, one of which is the actual abortion. So Planned Parenthood would say that abortion was only 25% of what they did for that woman, who came into the clinic only for an abortion.

It's like the NFL selling 5 million hot dogs in a season that had 256 games, and saying football is only .005% of what they do. Or like a steakhouse saying "steak is only a small percentage of what we serve, because we also serve salad, baked potatoes, french fries, beer, wine, and soda." They're still a steakhouse.[115] When you're in the business of murder, lying is easy. Even if the 3% figure were true, they are still responsible for over a third of a million deaths a year, and that makes them the largest abortion provider in the U.S. As we've also seen, abortion is an increasing percentage of what they do, compared to their other services.

In a fit of delusion, they fabricated the concept of a "war on women" in which conservatives and pro-lifers don't want women to have access to medical care. The only thing more ridiculous than this notion is the fact that they not only convinced themselves of this fairy tale, but tried to make it a public argument. No one in their right mind would deny anyone access to cancer screenings and STD tests. People who believe that a pregnancy is unborn human life object to being fed the lie that the violent destruction of a fetus is part of this "healthcare". Contrary to what anti-lifers would have us believe, those who support unborn life have no issue with women accessing *real* healthcare. But as we've seen previously, abortion is not healthcare.

The first edition of this book contained a proposition. "If Planned Parenthood really believes that they are in the healthcare business, let them prove it", and proposed the following challenge: that if they stopped doing abortions, which by their claims, make up only a miniscule percentage of their services anyway, then no one would call for defunding them and the closing of their clinics. Then in a March 6, 2017 New York Times article, Maggie Haberman describes how President Trump made that same proposal to Planned Parenthood and they declined, making the same exaggerated and weak argument touting all the non-abortion, beneficial medical screenings they supposedly do, and how no federal money goes to paying for abortions.

That last argument is also suspect, because money is fungible, i.e., it can be shifted from one expense to another. In this example, Planned Parenthood could easily use the hundreds of millions of dollars they receive yearly from taxpayers to fund advertising, utilities or rent on their facilities, and shift the money that would have gone for those expenses to abortion.

One of the many recent heroes in the pro-life movement is David Daleiden, who worked with Live Action before founding The Center For Medical Progress in 2013. Mr. Daleiden pulled back the curtain on one of the most heinous of Planned Parenthood's illegal activities: the sale of baby body parts. The tide began to turn against Planned Parenthood in 2015, when he filmed conversations with Planned Parenthood employees regarding the illegal sale of body parts from aborted babies. In these videos, which have been verified as "unedited" by independent, third party videography companies, we see and hear Planned Parenthood employees glibly but gruesomely explaining how to harvest intact organs from aborted babies, and how much money they can earn by selling these parts to medical research and experimentation companies. Providing fetal tissue for medical research is legal, but financially profiting from it is not.

In another Daleiden video, we see a Planned Parenthood abortionist joking about how she needs to do more arm workouts at the gym to be able to detach an arm or a leg from a live baby she's aborting.[116] Another abortionist is clearly heard on tape saying that she welcomes the money earned from the sale of baby body parts because she wants a Lamborghini.[117]

When Planned Parenthood abortionists were also caught on tape admitting that they sometimes have to "alter the procedure for financial gain", (also illegal) they were explaining how they abort a baby and still keep the marketable organs intact, which brings more money from medical researchers than a mangled organ.[118]

Of course, Planned Parenthood attacked Mr. Daleiden with a vengeance, and was helped in their court cases by anti-life politicians and judges whom they had supported. Daleiden had charged that a Gulf Coast chapter of Planned Parenthood was selling body parts of aborted babies. In January, 2016, a grand jury in Houston not only cleared Planned Parenthood of any wrongdoing, but incredibly, indicted Daleiden and the Center For Medical Progress on charges of emailing an offer to buy fetal tissue from Planned Parenthood. In obvious actuality, this was an attempt to obtain proof of Planned Parenthood's trafficking in baby body parts, not an attempt to actually participate in the sale of these parts. After Daleiden's legal team showed that the Harris County District Attorney's office colluded with Planned Parenthood lawyers, the charges were dropped.[119] [120]

In California, Mr. Daleiden has faced similar or worse persecution. In a January, 2019 interview with EWTN's Catherine Hadro, Daleiden explains how former California Attorney General Kamala Harris was relentless in her attempt to punish him and defend Planned Parenthood's interests, from whom she has received substantial campaign donations. In the interview, he recounts how Harris met repeatedly with Planned Parenthood officials. The California Attorney General's investigative case notes show that Planned Parenthood specifically requested that she have Daleiden's apartment ransacked in an attempt to confiscate any videos he had of Planned Parenthood's activities in California to traffic in aborted baby body parts. In April, 2016, eleven California Department of Justice officials, with a search warrant from Harris, overturned Daleiden's apartment, seizing all his electronic equipment. This attempted coverup of illegal Planned Parenthood activities in California would have been successful, had it not been for Daleiden previously having sent multiple copies of the videos to his attorneys. Asked what he would like the public to know about Kamala Harris in light of the fact that she was a 2020 presidential candidate, Daleiden describes only one of her hypocritical actions:

I just saw her recently on MSNBC talking about the confirmation hearings of William Barr, who's the nominee for attorney general, and Senator Harris was opining that nominee Barr, if confirmed, should recuse himself from the Russia investigation because of some op-eds he's written about the Mueller probe. When Kamala Harris had the Planned Parenthood case, which was the investigation of me, brought before her as attorney general while she was running for U.S. Senate, while Planned Parenthood in California was contributing to her political campaign and she was fundraising for them .... did she recuse herself from the Planned Parenthood investigation? No, she didn't, in fact, she didn't even set up ... they sometimes talk about having a 'wall of separation' in the prosecutor's office in order to make sure there's no improper crossover. Not only did she not recuse herself, not set up a wall of separation, she consciously and willfully involved herself directly and personally in the Planned Parenthood case. She had an in-person meeting with six Planned Parenthood executives from California, in Los Angeles, two weeks before the raid on my apartment. We have the action item notes, and the email from her assistant from that meeting. They show that among the Planned Parenthood folks present, two of them were witnesses in the criminal investigation that Kamala Harris' office was orchestrating against me and Sandra (Merritt) and they show that the agenda items that Kamala Harris discussed with those Planned Parenthood witnesses and reps at that meeting included both Planned Parenthood's political agenda in California and issues in the criminal investigation, so there was a direct mixing of her political roles and political agenda and campaign agenda and political agenda of an outside third party, directly mixed in, inseparable from her role as a law enforcement officer.[121]

The accusation against Planned Parenthood of "selling baby body parts" is merely the headline of the news articles. Reading these articles in their entirety reveals gruesome details that could have come from the most depraved of horror movies. Most abortions result in mangled pieces of fetuses. However, it is the intact organs that are most in demand by biomedical procurement and scientific experimental companies. In order to attain intact organs for sale, Planned Parenthood must resort to different, often illegal abortion procedures. These procedures usually require women to be over-dilated to ensure an extremely quick delivery of babies who are often born alive. In one of his court appearances in 2019, Daleiden explained how, at the Association of Reproductive Health Professionals conference in September, 2013, he met

Ruth Arrick, of Choice Pursuits, a consultant for abortion facilities who advised the investigators to find abortionists who don't ensure fetal demise before delivery. . . . Sandra Merritt was working as an undercover investigator at the conference along with Brianna Baxter. . . Merritt was using the name Susan Tennebaum, who was starting a tissue procurement company called BioMax and was looking to get in touch with abortion facility medical directors. Merritt and Baxter met Arrick there, who advised them to find doctors who were willing to over-dilate abortion patients, which she also admitted was a risk to the patients' health.

An audio clip of their conversation proved this shocking detail, along with other disturbing information. Arrick can be heard telling the undercover journalists that they should locate abortion clinics that weren't in the practice of using digoxin to kill the babies before they were delivered, mentioning the Feminist Women's Health Center and the Feminist Abortion Network site specifically. She stated that with digoxin, she 'knows when the baby's gonna die.' Without digoxin, babies could easily be born alive. She also can be heard in the recording mentioning Dr. David Gluck and his method of abortion which she described as: 'clamp the cord and just wait a minute or two. She also said they would be able to find facilities that commit abortion up to 24 weeks and don't use digoxin to ensure fetal death before live birth.[122]

The Center for Medical Progress website also describes the contents of the seventh video they filmed.

The third episode in a new documentary web series and seventh video on Planned Parenthood's supply of aborted fetal tissue tells a former procurement technician's har-rowing story of harvesting an intact brain from a late-term male fetus whose heart was still beating after the abortion.

The 'Human Capital' documentary web series, produced by The Center For Medical Progress, integrates expert interviews, eyewitness accounts, and real-life undercover interactions to explore different themes within Planned Parenthood's sale of aborted fetal tissue. Episode Three, 'Planned Parenthood's Custom Abortions for Superior Product,' launches today at:http:// www.centerformedicalprogress.org/2015/08/ human-capital-episode-3-planned-parent- hoods-custom-abortions-for-superior-product/

The series focuses on the personal narrative of Holly O'Donnell, a former Blood and Tissue Procurement Technician for StemExpress, a biotech start-up that until last week was part-nered with two large northern California Planned Parenthood affiliates to purchase their aborted fetus parts and resell them for scientific experimentation.

O'Donnell describes the harvesting, or 'pro-curement,' of organs from a nearly intact late-term fetus aborted at Planned Parenthood Mar Monte's Alameda clinic in San Jose, CA. '. . . want to see some-thing kind of cool?' O'Donnell says her supervisor asked her. 'And she just taps the heart, and it starts beating. And I'm sitting here and I'm looking at this fetus, and its heart is beating, and I don't know what to think.'

The San Jose Planned Parenthood does abortions up to 20 weeks of pregnancy. Referring to the beating heart of the aborted fetus, O'Donnell remarks, 'I don't know if that constitutes it's technically dead, or it's alive.'

California law prohibits any kind of experimentation on a fetus with a discernible heartbeat (CA Health and Safety Code 123440). StemExpress has been cited in published scientific literature as a source of fetal hearts used for Langendorff perfusion, which keeps a heart beating after it is excised from the body: http://www.hindawi. com/journals/omcl/2015/730683/

O'Donnell also tells how her StemExpress supervisor instructed her to cut through the face of the fetus in order to get the brain. 'She gave me the scissors and told me that I had to cut down the middle of the face. I can't even describe what that feels like,' she says.

The video also features recordings of Dr. Ben Van Handel, the Executive Director of Novogenix Laboratories, LLC, and also of Perrin Larton, Procurement Manager of Advanced Bioscience Resources, Inc. (ABR). Novogenix is the company that has harvested fetal organs from abortions done by Planned Parenthood Federation of America's Senior Director of Medical Services, Dr. Deborah Nucatola, in Los Angeles, while ABR is the oldest fetal tissue procurement company and works with Planned Parenthood in San

Diego and other clinics around the country. Van Handel admits, 'There are times when after the procedure is done that the heart actually is still beating,' and Larton describes abortions she has seen where 'the fetus was already in the vaginal canal whenever we put her in the stirrups, it just fell out.'

CMP's Project Lead David Daleiden notes, 'Today's video contains heart rending admissions about the absolute barbarism of Planned Parenthood's abortion practice and baby parts sales in which fetuses are sometimes delivered intact and alive. Planned Parenthood is a criminal organization from the top down and should be immediately stripped of taxpayer funding and prosecuted for their atrocities against humanity.'[123]

As if all this weren't enough, it turns out that Planned Parenthood is the best friend of sex traffickers of young girls. Multiple sources, some of which used undercover video techniques similar to David Daleidan's, detail how that instead of reporting sexual abuse and trafficking of minors to the proper authorities as required by law, Planned Parenthood instead cooperated with traffickers in providing contraceptives and abortions to victims of sexual abuse and trafficking.

Live Action, the investigative group that released the undercover footage in 2011, has a new report alleging that cover up of child sexual abuse and sex trafficking at Planned Parenthood has taken place at locations across the country.

The report, titled 'Aiding Abusers: Planned Parenthood's Cover-Up of Child Sexual Abuse' features nearly two decades worth of research and contains testimonials from former Planned Parenthood employees, court cases where Planned Parenthood was accused of negligence in failing to report suspected abuse, undercover video footage from prior investigations, and statements from women whose abuse was not reported to authorities by Planned Parenthood.

The report cites numerous examples of girls who were under the age of consent and brought to a clinic for an abortion. Girls as young as 12 and 13 received abortions, which were not reported to authorities, Live Action said.

A 2014 study by Loyola University Chicago's Beazley Institute for Health and Law Policy found that aside from emergency rooms, Planned Parenthood locations were the most-visited facilities by trafficking victims. One trafficking victim interviewed for that report said that Planned Parenthood 'didn't ask any questions' that would have revealed the abuse.[124]

In addition, the Washington Post reported in January, 2017, that

Live Action released Tuesday a new video featuring former Planned Parenthood clinic manager Ramona Trevino, who was still employed by the abortion provider when the first undercover videos were released in 2011. Contrary to what Planned Parenthood told the media at the time, Ms. Trevino said the abortion provider responded to the videos — not by training employees how to spot and report sextrafficking — but by teaching them how not to get caught saying incriminating things to undercover journalists.

'I couldn't believe that we were actually there to train on how to identify if we're being recorded, Ms. Trevino says in the six-minute video. 'Again, it goes back to, do we have something to hide? Why is this an issue for us?' It was an eye-opening moment for Ms. Trevino, who said she resigned out of disgust.

'That experience left me so disgusted that I couldn't see how Planned Parenthood could ever redeem themselves after that,' she said.

Live Action's 2011 investigation caught on camera eight Planned Parenthood workers at seven facilities who were willing to help a man who identified himself as a sex trafficker covertly obtain abortions and other reproductive health care services for minors as young as 14.

In one of the videos, the actor posing as the pimp asks a Planned Parenthood clinician how long his workers would have to wait before returning to work after obtaining an abortion. When the clinician responds that they could not be sexually active for at least two weeks, the man inquires as to whether they could do anything else during that time, because 'they still gotta make money, you know?' 'Waist up,' the Planned Parenthood employee says. 'Waist up. Or just be that extra action walking by.'

Much like the 2015 Center for Medical Progress videos alleging Planned Parenthood traffics in fetal body parts from abortions, the Live Action videos became a national scandal, prompting House Republicans, led by then-Rep. Mike Pence, to seek to defund Planned Parenthood.

Despite the publicity surrounding the video investigation, Live Action founder Lila Rose said Planned Parenthood never took its results seriously. 'Well, Planned Parenthood's response to the fact that seven of their facilities and high-level staffers were caught on tape aiding and abetting child sex trafficking was more of the same,' Ms. Rose said. 'Instead of solving the problem, they lied to cover up the problem further.'

After the videos surfaced in early 2011, Planned Parenthood Federation of America President Cecile Richards sent a letter to then-Attorney General Eric H. Holder Jr. telling him the abortion provider would 'comply with applicable state laws relating to reporting of suspected instances of conduct that endangers the welfare of minors.'

But Live Action filed Freedom of Information Act requests with justice, police and child services departments in the five jurisdictions — Arizona, New Jersey, New York, Virginia and Washington, D.C. — where the investigation was conducted. It could find evidence that Planned Parenthood contacted authorities only in Arizona.

Planned Parenthood could not be reached for comment. Ms. Rose said the absence of a more robust paper trail indicates Planned Parenthood tried not only to 'aid and abet sex traffickers, but they also did not report them to authorities as they claimed to.'[125]

Let's pause for a moment at this point to discuss a phenomenon I call a different take on "the deer in the headlights look." This is something Kristan Hawkins of Students For Life also similarly described in early 2020. When a pro-life person who has researched the barbaric horrors and the seamy underside of the abortion industry begins to share these gruesome details, people give them that "deer in the headlights" look of shocked disbelief. Even some other pro-life people hearing these things think "what this extremist is telling me is too horrific to be true; this can't be happening in the United States."

There are two reasons for this reaction that are actually quite understandable. The first is that these details actually sound like something from a bad science fiction movie that couldn't possibly be connected to reality, and second, it resembles nothing they have ever heard before because the biased mainstream media in the U.S. has never reported on anything that casts their ally Planned Parenthood in a negative light.

An idea that has never existed in the human mind is not easily absorbed and comprehended when first encountered, i.e., a conversation from 500 years ago: "What do you mean

Magellan sailed around the world? He had to have fallen off the edge." Or a contemporary example: "Yea, I just got back from 1842, had dinner with my great-great-great grandparents. It was a great time." What?

Planned Parenthood's website sings the praises of Margaret Sanger who "founded the American birth control movement and, later, the Planned Parenthood Federation of America". Planned Parenthood's website is full of their devotion to the woman who has so greatly inspired them. It describes their "highest honor, the Planned Parenthood Federation of America Margaret Sanger Award". In New York, one of their largest clinics is the Margaret Sanger Center. They laud her in a small biography "Margaret Sanger – 20th Century Hero." They praise her "outreach to the African-American community." But a closer look reveals a dark side of Planned Parenthood's founder, who had some offensive things to say about race and birth control. An outspoken eugenicist, Sanger consistently made racist claims. From her December, 1939 letter to Dr. Clarence Gamble of Milton, Massachusetts:

> We should hire three or four colored ministers, preferably with social-service backgrounds, and with engaging personalities. The most successful educational approach to the Negro is through a religious appeal. We don't want the word to go out that we want to exterminate the Negro population, and the minister is the man who can straighten out that idea if it ever occurs to any of their more rebellious members.[126]

The following is just one illustration of the verbal gymnastics Planned Parenthood goes to in order to cast Sanger in a positive light. In an attempt to defend the above statement "We do not want word to get out that we want to exterminate the Negro population", Planned Parenthood's website states that "a larger portion of the letter makes Sanger's meaning clear:"

> It seems to me from my experience ... that while the colored Negroes have great respect for white doctors, they can get closer to their own members and more or less lay their cards on the table ... They do not do this with the white people, and if we can train the Negro doctor at the clinic, he can go among them with enthusiasm and with knowledge, which I believe, will have far-reaching results.[113]

However, they still conveniently omit portions of the quote which are inconvenient to their purposes. The words deleted in the second ellipsis actually were "which means their ignorance, superstitions and doubts."[127]

In her article "Plan for Peace" from the April, 1932 edition of the *Birth Control Review*, Sanger states that we should "apply a stern and rigid policy of sterilization and segregation to that grade of population whose progeny is tainted, or whose inheritance is such that objectionable traits may be transmitted to offspring."[128]

Another point she recommended was "to keep the doors of immigration closed to the entrance of certain aliens whose condition is known to be detrimental to the stamina of the race" because as she noted in *Woman, Morality, and Birth Control* in 1922, "Birth control must lead ultimately to a cleaner race."[128]

In "Pivot of Civilization" from 1922, Sanger explains her eugenic philosophy of the types of inferior people she believes should not be allowed to exist:

Such parents swell the pathetic ranks of the unemployed. Feeble-mindedness perpetuates itself from the ranks of those who are blandly indifferent to their racial responsibilities. And it is largely this type of humanity we are now drawing upon to populate our world for the generations to come. In this orgy of multiplying and replenishing the earth, this type is *pari passu* multiplying and perpetuating those direst evils in which we must, if civilization is to survive, extirpate by the very roots.

They are...human weeds, reckless breeders, spawning... human beings who never should have been born. Organized charity itself is the symptom of a malignant social disease...

Instead of decreasing and aiming to eliminate the stocks [of people] that are most detrimental to the future of the race and the world, it tends to render them to a menacing degree dominant.

Our failure to segregate morons who are increasing and multiplying ...demonstrates our foolhardy and extravagant sentimentalism ... [Philanthropists] encourage the healthier and more normal sections of the world to shoulder the burden of unthinking and indiscriminate fecundity of others, which brings with it, as I think the reader must agree, a dead weight of human waste.

Instead of decreasing and aiming to eliminate the stocks that are most detrimental to the future of the race and the world, it tends to render them to a menacing degree dominant ... We are paying for, and even submitting to, the dictates of an ever-increasing, unceasingly spawning class of human beings who never should have been born at all.[129]

A detail the pro-death proponents will never allow brought to light is that in May, 1926, Margaret Sanger accepted an invitation to speak to the women's branch of the Ku Klux Klan in Silver Lake, New Jersey. On page 366 of her 1938 autobiography, she proclaims that

I accepted an invitation to talk to the women's branch of the Ku Klux Klan ... I saw through the door dim figures parading with banners and illuminated crosses ... I was escorted to the platform, was introduced, and began to speak ... In the end, through simple illustrations I believed I had accomplished my purpose. A dozen invitations to speak to similar groups were proffered.[130]

In a 1957 interview with journalist Mike Wallace, Sanger advocated that the greatest evil is a family that chooses to bring certain children into the world.

I think the greatest sin in the world is bringing children into the world that have disease from their parents, that have no chance in the world to be a human being practically. Delinquents, prisoners, all sorts of things just marked when they're born. That to me is the greatest sin that people can commit.[131]

One of Sanger's favorite slogans, found at the top of her *Birth Control Review*, was: "Birth Control: To Create a Race of Thoroughbreds."Live Action also clearly ties Planned Parenthood with its founder:

> Sanger's disdain for blacks, minority groups, and the diseased and disabled spawned the birth of an abortion corporation that profits off the killing of the weakest and most vulnerable. Today, the spirit of Sanger lives on. According to the Guttmacher Institute, African-American women are five times more likely to choose abortion over white women. Planned Parenthood clinics are strategically planted in minority communities, targeting blacks and impoverished minority groups, and abortion remains the leading cause of death for the black community.[132]

Live Action goes on to describe how Sanger

> initiated the Negro Project to weed out the unfit from the black population. In bringing birth control to the then largely poor (i.e. unfit) population of the South, with a few influential black ministers promoting the project as the solution to poverty, Sanger hoped to significantly reduce the black population. Martin Luther King, Sr., as the eldest son of nine children born into poverty in a family of sharecroppers, would have made

the perfect target for' elimination.' But his birth had already taken place.[133]

Fr. Robert Barron, one of the leading theologians and philosophers of our time reveals an unnerving truth: that these racist eugenic ideas are still alive today, of all places, on the current Supreme Court:

> Margaret Sanger . . . felt that people of low quality—and for her this meant non-whites—were reproducing at far too high a rate and that these unpromising types should be prevented, if need be forcibly—from passing on their genes.

> One might be forgiven for thinking that this sort of attitude is a relic of the distant past, but consider this. In 2009, Supreme Court Justice Ruth Bader Ginsburg was granted an interview with The New York Times Magazine. In the course of the conversation, she turned to a consideration of the Hyde Amendment which blocks Medicaid from funding abortions, and she said, 'Frankly I had thought that at the time Roe was decided, there was concern about population growth and particularly growth in populations that we don't want to have too many of...'

> One wonders just who Justice Ginsburg thinks these undesirables might be. If nearly two-thirds of black women's pregnancies are ending in abortion, are we not justified in concluding that Margaret Sanger's racist fantasy has come true?[134]

Planned Parenthood and other pro-death supporters wish that some of the more open-minded feminists who dare to question abortion were less vocal with their opinions. According to Schwarzwalder and Ruse:

> 'Pro-choice' feminist Naomi Wolf, in a ground-breaking article in 1996, argued that the abortion-rights community should acknowledge the 'fetus, in its full humanity' and that abortion causes 'a real death.'[135] More recently, Kate Michelman, long-time president of NARAL Pro-Choice America, acknowledged that 'technology has clearly helped to define how people think about a fetus as a full, breathing human being.'[136]

> Roe-era feminists like Kate Michelman, the former president of NARALPro-Choice America, proclaimed abortion to be 'the guarantor of a woman's right to participate fully in the social and political life of society.[137] But pro-life feminists believe this turns feminism on its head because it says women don't have an inherent right to participate in society, but one conditioned on surgery and sacrificing their children.

> No women should have to abort her child to participate fully in society. If a pregnant woman or mother can't participate in society, the true feminist response is that something is wrong with society.

> It is also at odds with the views of America's first feminists, all of whom opposed abortion.

Chief among them were Susan B. Anthony and Elizabeth Cady Stanton, who not only led the fight for the right of women to own property, to vote, and obtain equal education, but also spoke out against abortion.

Susan B. Anthony's newspaper, The Revolution, called abortion 'child murder' and 'infanticide.'[138] In 1869 Anthony said: 'No matter what the motive, love of ease, or a desire to save from suffering the unborn innocent, the woman is awfully guilty who commits the deed. It will burden her conscience in life, it will burden her soul in death; But oh, thrice guilty is he who drove her to the desperation which impelled her to the crime!'[139]

Casey Maddox, senior counsel lawyer for the Alliance Defending Freedom and member of the bar of the U.S. Supreme Court, writes in his 2012 article "Eleven Thousand Reasons Why Planned Parenthood Can't Be Trusted":

For the past five years, every dawn has brought additional evidence of the fact that Planned Parenthood and its allies in the abortion industry cannot be trusted to tell the truth about the one thing they should know well – abortion. Just over five years ago, on April 18, 2007, the Supreme Court announced its opinion in *Gonzales v. Carhart*, holding that the federal Partial-Birth Abortion Ban Act was constitutional. Since then, we have lived in a world where partial-birth abortions have been illegal in the United States under federal law (and now many state laws).

Yet the most valuable part of the *Gonzales* opinion may not be its upholding of the PBA Ban, but the fact that it called the abortion industry's bluff. And history has now demonstrated that Planned Parenthood and its allies were holding a joker.

The *Gonzales* decision held that the federal ban on partial-birth abortions, except where necessary to save a woman's life, was facially constitutional – meaning that generally speaking, the ban was constitutionally sound. Opponents of the ban, including Planned Parenthood and their allies, had argued strenuously that the law was unconstitutional because it lacked a 'health' exception. The Guttmacher Institute, Planned Parenthood's *de facto* research arm, claimed that roughly 2,200 (probably a low estimate) occurred in a representative year prior to the ban – almost all of which were performed because they were necessary to protect a woman's health.

Congress had omitted the exception because of evidence that such an exception was not necessary in practice and that such an exception would merely be used to circumvent the law entirely, with abortionists claiming falsely that virtually every partial-birth abortion was necessary for 'health' reasons, and in *Doe v. Bolton*, the companion case to *Roe v. Wade*, the court had created a health exemption so wide that it covered just about everything including depression.

Congress's judgment was buttressed by a statement from the American Medical Association that partial-birth abortion was 'not medically indicated.' Indeed, the American College of Obstetricians and Gynecologists also agreed that partial-birth abortion was virtually never (if ever) necessary. Before then Solicitor General Kagan intervened to prevent what she called 'a disaster' and proposed alternative language for ACOG in its written testimony to Congress.

The Court didn't have to decide that a health exception was always unnecessary as a factual matter, deferring to Congress's judgment on the matter. It simply refused to declare the whole law unconstitutional because of the theoretical possibility that a woman might need an abortion for a non-life-threatening health reason. But importantly, the Court held that abortionists could bring future challenges to the law on behalf of actual women who needed a partial-birth abortion for true health reasons.

Hours after the decision, Planned Parenthood was still warning of its imminent negative impact on women's health. The battle seemingly joined, Justice Ginsburg's dissenting opinion, citing the ACOG/Kagan language, specifically invited as-applied challenges on behalf of the alleged thousands of women who needed the partial-birth abortion procedure for health reasons: 'One may anticipate that such a preenforcement challenge will be mounted swiftly, to ward off serious, sometimes irremediable harm, to women whose health would be endangered by the intact D&E prohibition.'

Over five years later, Justice Ginsburg and the nation still wait. Although women's health was allegedly immediately harmed by the decision, we have not yet seen an as-applied challenge on behalf of one of these women, nor have we seen even one documented story of a woman whose health was impacted by the unavailability of a partial-birth abortion. If we accept Guttmacher's figure of approximately 2,200 partial-birth abortions per year, then the decision in *Gonzales* – upholding the law and lifting the injunction against it – has prevented 11,000 partial-birth abortions from occurring.

And recall that the argument was that this one procedure was the only way to protect a woman's health. It was *necessary*, we were told. And yet, there is no evidence whatsoever that any woman's health has been harmed by the unavailability of this procedure. No as-applied challenge as invited by Justice Ginsburg, no *Newsweek* cover story, no *Rachel Maddow Show* interview of a woman whose identity is hidden, no *Journal of the American Medical Association* article, nothing.

What are we to believe now that we have over five years of a lack of such evidence? I see four options:

(1) Planned Parenthood and its allies were being truthful, and up until April 18, 2007, approximately six partial-birth abortions per day were performed for health reasons – but by an incredible blessing, those health threats ceased on that morning until the present. I'll call this the "dispensational" argument.

(2) Planned Parenthood and its allies were correct, and women have been harmed by the *Gonzales* decision, but the abortion lobby lacks the financial and legal resources to file a challenge on behalf of one of these thousands of women.

(3) The abortion industry continues to perform partial-birth abortions in violation of federal law.

(4) The claim by Planned Parenthood and its allies that partial-birth abortions were – and are – necessary to protect women's health is untrue.

Draw your own conclusions about which of these is the more likely explanation. But should it surprise us that Planned Parenthood and its abortion industry allies are willing to lie and distort the facts in order to protect their sacred (and coincidentally – cash) cow? With roughly $8 million in documented waste, abuse, and potential fraud in just a few Planned Parenthood affiliates – should we be surprised?

For more than five years, every day has brought more evidence to answer this question. Will

Planned Parenthood and its abortion industry allies lie about 'women's health' in order to further their ideology of death and support their bottom line? As surely as the sun rises in the east.[140]

Cal Thomas, a columnist with the Chicago Tribune also writes of an example of Planned Parenthood being a little more than disingenuous:

To maintain a policy of abortion on demand, proponents have had to continue telling lies. Planned Parenthood, which consistently argues for maintaining the abortion status quo, once told a different story. In 1965, a Planned Parenthood pamphlet called 'Plan Your Children' said of family planning: Is it abortion? Definitely not. An abortion kills the life of a baby after it has begun. It is dangerous to your life and health. It may make you sterile so that when you want a child you cannot have it. Birth control merely postpones the beginning of life.' Was Planned Parenthood lying then, or is it lying now?[141]

Planned Parenthood's website also makes reference to civil rights leader Dr. Martin Luther King, suggesting he was a great supporter of their activities. However, King's niece, Dr. Alveda King, described Planned Parenthood's deceit in the African American community and puts in perspective her uncle's pro-life beliefs:

The most obvious practitioner of racism in the United States today is Planned Parenthood, an organization founded by the eugenicist Margaret Sanger and recently documented as ready to accept money to eliminate black babies.[142]

She goes on to state that

Planned Parenthood is no stranger to deception . . . Planned Parenthood lies by trying to imply that my uncle, Dr. Martin Luther King, Jr., would somehow endorse the organization today. He most certainly would not.

Uncle Martin accepted an award from Planned Parenthood in 1966 when abortion was illegal in every state and before Planned Parenthood started publicly advocating for it, continued Dr. King. In Planned Parenthood's own citation for Uncle Martin's prize, not only is no mention of abortion made, it states that 'human life and progress are indeed indivisible.' In 1966, neither the general public nor my uncle was aware of the true agenda of Planned Parenthood, an agenda of death that has become painfully obvious as the years have unfolded.

Dr. Martin Luther King, Jr., said, 'The Negro cannot win if he is willing to sacrifice the future of his children for personal comfort and safety,' and 'Injustice anywhere is a threat to injustice everywhere,' added Dr. King. 'There is no way he would want his name or image associated today with Planned Parenthood, the group most responsible for denying civil rights to the over

45 million American babies killed by abortion, one-third of them African-American. There is no way my uncle would condone the violence of abortion, violence that Planned Parenthood has always tried to mask, which brings painful deaths to babies and can result in torn wombs, serious infections, and emotional devastation for their mothers. Let me be clear, Planned Parenthood must stop using and lying to my family and the entire community of humanity."[143]

The Corona virus pandemic of early 2020 brought Planned Parenthood's rabid devotion to abortion into the light of day in the most transparent way. As more and more businesses, schools and public spaces were closed during March, 2020 in an attempt to stop the spread of the virus, the great majority of Planned Parenthood facilities remained open for business, sometimes in direct violation of government orders. By staying open, they made the public statement that they were willing to put their patients and employees at risk for contracting the virus and spreading it to the larger public in order to continue to make profits and reach their abortion quotas, using needed medical supplies that could have been used to treat patients with the virus. Some facilities temporarily eliminated the few non-abortion services they offered, rendering them abortion-only facilities. They even had the gall to ask for donations of more masks and other medical supplies.

The "elephant in the room" observation that pro-life advocates made (that Planned Parenthood ignored, hoping it would go away), was the issue of what constituted necessary, essential medical care. Alexis McGill Johnson, then acting president of Planned Parenthood, called abortion a "essential, time-sensitive medical procedure." Pro-life Texas Attorney General Ken Paxton pushed back, pointing out

> that abortion advocates have repeatedly main-
> tained that abortion is a 'choice' and should
> thus be considered an elective procedure, not
> an essential one. It is unconscionable that abor-
> tion providers are fighting against the health of
> Texans and withholding desperately needed sup-
> plies and personal protective equipment in favor
> of a procedure that they refer to as a 'choice'.[144]

Planned Parenthood could also not answer the question, "If abortion is an essential, necessary medical procedure, what disease or illness does it treat?" This question is answered thoroughly by Dr. James Studnicki, who

> over a span of four decades, (has) held aca-
> demic appointments at the Johns Hopkins
> University School of Hygiene and Public Health,
> the University of South Florida College of Public
> Health, and the University of North Carolina,
> Charlotte, where for ten years he served as the
> Irwin Belk Endowed Chair in Health Services
> Research. Studnicki holds Doctor of Science
> (ScD) and Master of Public Health (MPH)
> degrees from Johns Hopkins and a Master of
> Business Administration (MBA) from the George
> Washington University.[145]

Dr. Studnicki's article published in April, 2019 in the Journal of Health Services Research and Managerial Epidemiology states that

If an induced abortion is healthcare, still a widely debated question, then the procedure must meet the requirements of being medically necessary. Exempting abortion from the test of medical necessity essentially relinquishes any claim that it is health care. While the concept of medical necessity has been defined in myriad ways, a few key elements present in all of the definitions across a range of medical specialties are especially relevant in the context of induced abortion:

1. The service must be required to prevent, diagnose, or treat an illness, injury, or disease. Pregnancy is neither an illness nor a disease and, following conception, is no longer preventable. Therefore, the treatment (abortion) must target another specified illness, injury, or disease.

2. The service must be clinically appropriate and considered effective for the individual illness, injury, or disease. This requirement implies that credible, evidence-based peer-reviewed literature exists that the abortion procedure will produce a positive result on specified outcomes related to the pregnant woman's illness, injury, or disease. In many states, the official language of the medical necessity determination form is too vague to allow such treatment- to-outcome specificity. In New Jersey, for example, physicians may consider 'physical, emotional, and psychological factors' in determining whether a termination of pregnancy is medically necessary. There are specific clinical criteria available

for determining the medical necessity for psychiatric treatment: a diagnosed disorder; which can be improved by the treatment based on accepted medical standards; presence of the illness documented by *Diagnostic and Statistical Manual of Mental Disorders* (Fifth Edition) codes assigned; and determination made by a licensed mental health professional.[9] Too often, these assessments are neglected or superficially completed using inappropriate documentation and by persons without appropriate credentials and experience.[10]

3. The service is not primarily for the convenience of the individual, the individual's health-care provider, or other health-care providers.[145]

In other words, for a procedure to qualify as true "health care", it should meet the three requirements Dr. Studnicki describes above. Point one is self-explanatory: "The service (in this case abortion) must be required to prevent, diagnose or treat an illness, injury or disease. Pregnancy is neither an illness nor a disease." In point two, the "service must be clinically appropriate and considered effective for the individual illness, injury, or disease." He discusses the effect of pregnancy on emotional and mental health, but cites problems in assessing these conditions. Knowing what abortion really is draws point three into sharp focus: abortionists' own data show that almost all abortions *are* "for the convenience of the individual," and in view of the fact that abortionists are financially profiting from abortions, are also convenient for them.

Chapter 11–Who have we aborted?

No, I don't miss you . . . Not in a way that one is missed. But I think of you. Sometimes. In the way that one might think of the summer sunshine on a winter night . . . – Sreesha Divakaran

T he next time you attend a meeting of any group you belong to, the next time you go to a sporting event, concert, church, class, or any event in public, look around you. Depending on the age group, between one fourth and one fifth of the people who should be there are missing. They didn't have a schedule conflict, they weren't sick, it's not that they weren't interested enough to attend, or are out of town. They're not in attendance because they were aborted. The 61 million Americans lost to abortion accounts for approximately one fifth of what would have been our total population had they not been killed.

Consider this: according to U.S. census figures, there were 3,612,000 live births in the United States in 1980.[146] There also were 1,553,900 abortions that year.[147] These figures yield an astounding fact: in 1980, over 30 percent of pregnancies in the United States ended in abortion. To illustrate who we have aborted, let us consider that of those 3,612,000 babies allowed to be born in 1980, approximately 17,400, or .48 percent, went on to be graduated from medical school as physicians, according to data from the Association of American Medical Colleges. Assuming that the percentage of those aborted would also have had a medical school graduation rate of .48 percent, we aborted approximately 7,459 future doctors in 1980 alone.

Considering the same statistical method, more questions become obvious: How many medical researchers have we aborted? Among those we aborted was there the one who would have found a cure for cancer, Alzheimer's, HIV or climate change? How many Nobel Prize winners and Olympic athletes were among the 61 million Americans we have killed to date? How many engineers, scientists, artists, and a multitude of others who would have contributed to the betterment of society have been lost? Those aborted in 1973 would be in their 40s today. How many would have helped build a more peaceful world?

On a more personal level, how many of those lost would have been our siblings, aunts, uncles, or cousins? The 61 million Americans aborted so far would have had childhoods, careers, homes, and possibly families of their own. They would have been our neighbors, co-workers, friends, and/or spouses. Those who would have been their children are the second, lost generation of abortion, and soon we will start to sense the loss of their grandchildren, the lost third generation. The loss of talent, value, and human potential to our society is staggering.

Chapter 12 – Religion and abortion

Have no fear about moving into the unknown. Simply step out fearlessly knowing that I am with you, therefore no harm can befall you ... Do this in complete faith and confidence.–Saint John Paul II

U ntil now, we have not mentioned the role religion plays in abortion. For people of faith, religion obviously takes center stage in the abortion debate. However, we live in a society that is becoming increasingly secular, and in fact, more and more hostile to religion. Statistics from every major poll show a continuing decrease in religious belief and participation over the last several decades. Gallup reported in December of 2017 that 33% of respondents in their poll self-identified as "not religious at all". Studies from a 2014 Pew Research Center poll tell us that 30% of the American public seldom or never attends any kind of church service, while another 33% attends either once or twice a month, or a few times a year.

In addition, the increase in open hostility and attacks on religious freedom in the United States has skyrocketed in the last few years. In the 2017 edition of "The Survey of Hostility to Religion in America", published by The First Liberty Institute and entitled "Undeniable", we learn that during the Obama years, from 2011 to 2016, there was a 133% increase in the attacks on religious liberty in the United States.[148]

For this reason, when engaged in a debate on abortion with an atheist or agnostic person, if the pro-life person frames the issue in a religious context, he or she has immediately lost the argument. In these cases, the two sides are no longer speaking the same language. The atheist has no frame of reference in which to consider the role religion plays in abortion, and couldn't care less whether the Bible supports innocent human life, or whether one of the 10 commandments is "Thou shalt not kill".

Therefore, when making the case for life when dialoging with an atheist, it is best to play their ball game in their stadium, by their rules. This means using logic and scientific fact to hopefully make them honestly reflect on the issue and consider that abortion is the slaughter of innocent human life. This book has provided just some of the enormous amount of logical, scientific, moral, legal, and philosophical proof that supports the pro-life argument.

The attacks on religious liberty go hand in hand with the attack on pro-life people and principles, since for most religions, abortion is an issue with obvious moral and theological implications. Almost every organized religion in the world values life. It is perhaps the only moral and theological issue on which almost all world religions generally agree. Judeo-Christian religions have valued life for thousands of years, including unborn human life.

The Society for the Protection of Unborn Children in London sums up the philosophies on abortion from the world's major religions.

The Catholic Church

The Catholic Church opposes abortion because it believes that life is sacred and inviolable. In 1995, Pope John Paul II wrote an encyclical letter called *Evangelium Vitae* (the Gospel of Life) in which he spoke of 'the sacred value of human life from its very beginning' and of the struggle between the culture of life and the culture of death.

The Orthodox Churches

Generally, the Orthodox Churches forbid abortion as going against the commandment 'Thou shalt not kill'. The Russian Orthodox Church condemned abortion in its *The Church and the Nation* published in 2000.

Protestant denominations

Most Protestant and Evangelical Christians are against abortion. In Northern Ireland, Catholics and Protestants have united against abortion. However, some denominations are more pro-abortion. The Church of England states that the unborn child is alive and created by God. The 1993 General Synod stated that 'the number of abortions carried out since the passage of the Abortion Act of 1967 is unacceptably high.' However, the Church of England also believes that abortion is sometimes morally acceptable such as when a baby is suffering from a serious disability.

Islam

Islam teaches that life begins at conception and is created by God. The unborn child has certain rights such as the right to care, protection and life. Abortion on any grounds is forbidden in the Islamic holy book *Al'Quran*. 'Do not kill or take a human life which God has declared to be sacred.' (Chapter 6, verse 151)

Judaism

The *Torah* or Jewish law forbids the taking of innocent life and stresses that human beings are made in the image of God. Maimonides, a twelfth century interpreter of Jewish law declared: 'A descendent of Noah who kills any human being, even a fetus in its mother's womb, is to be put to death. The only exception was if the mother's life was in danger. . . .

Hinduism

Hindu scriptures refer to abortion as *garha-batta* (womb killing) and the *Atharva Veda* describes abortionists as the greatest of sinners. Gandhi, perhaps the most respected Hindu of the twentieth century, said: 'It seems to me clear as daylight that abortion would be a crime.'[149]

In Luke's Gospel, Jesus and John the Baptist "greet" one another while they are still in their mothers' wombs. Verse 41 of the first chapter says: "It happened, when Elizabeth heard

Mary's greeting, the baby leaped in her womb, and Elizabeth was filled with the Holy Spirit."

Psalm 139 describes the development of the unborn baby:

> For you created my inmost being, you knit me together in my mother's womb. I praise you because I am fearfully and wonderfully made; your works are wonderful, I know that full well. My frame was not hidden from you when I was made in the secret place. When I was woven together in the depths of the earth, your eyes saw my unformed body.

One of the earliest Christian writings, the Didache, or the Teaching of the Twelve Apostles, states: "You shall not kill the child in the womb or murder a new-born infant."[150]The prophet Jeremiah wrote in his first chapter, verses 4-5: "Then the word of the Lord came to me, saying: "Before I formed you in the womb I knew you; before you were born I sanctified you; I ordained you a prophet to the nations." Job wrote in chapter 31, verses 14-15: "What then shall I do when God rises up? When He punishes, how shall I answer Him? Did not He who made me in the womb make them? Did not the same One fashion us in the womb?" Luke 1:15 states that John the Baptist will be "filled with the Holy Spirit, even from his mother's womb," which means that the baby in the womb has a soul for the Holy Spirit to fill.

"Thou shalt not kill" is one of the ten Commandments. What anti-lifers are proposing, in effect, is to dispose of one of the ten Commandments. A person would have to be either an atheist or a colossal egomaniac to feel entitled and worthy of altering the ten Commandments.

All the more mystifying, therefore, are those who supposedly call themselves religious, yet defend the killing of God's most defenseless life. What kind of mental and philosophical gymnastics must groups like "Catholics for Choice" and liberal politicians who call themselves "religious" have to go through to convince themselves that they can be religious and also support abortion? They live in a delusional world where their own arrogance justifies them playing God, appointing themselves as the determiners of what is morally acceptable and what is not; of who lives and who dies. As Father Flannigan, a character in the 1940's film "Boys Town" said: "life and death should be left to the creator of life and death."

In the few times pro-death advocates mention the bible, they claim that it contains no mention of abortion. Kerby Anderson, president of Probe Ministries International and nationally syndicated columnist explains that . . .

> the Bible doesn't say anything about abortion directly. Why the silence of the Bible on abortion? The answer is simple. Abortion was so unthinkable to an Israelite woman that there was no need to even mention it in the criminal code. Why was abortion an unthinkable act? First, children were viewed as a gift or heritage from the Lord. Second, the Scriptures state—and the Jews concurred—that God opens and closes the womb and is sovereign over conception. Third, childlessness was seen as a curse.[151]

Hispanics have a long and intimate spiritual tradition as Catholics that goes back 500 years. Now being the largest ethnic minority in the United States, they clearly have the power to live one of the basic tenets of their faith, and help change the culture of death in this country to a culture of life. They have a tremendous opportunity to wield their political power in favor of protecting the unborn. It is quite possible that their support for pro-life political candidates could turn the tide in making abortion illegal in the United States.

However, the sad reality is that once assimilated to the culture of their new country, they often abandon their religious heritage in favor of a political party that promotes the killing of the unborn. What political issues are more important than speaking up for the rights of those who cannot defend themselves; than protecting the lives of hundreds of thousands of innocents who are slaughtered every year in the United States?

A 2018 survey by the Pew Research Center/Religion and Public Life shows that only 44% of Hispanics believe abortion should be illegal in all or most cases, (and that percentage is dropping over time).[152] A separate Pew study found that in the mid-term elections of 2018, 69% of Hispanics voted for the Democratic (anti-life) candidate.[153]

We have already seen how science and religion don't need to be mutually exclusive. The eminent geneticist Francis Collins, M.D., Ph.D., and recipient of the Presidential Medal of Freedom for his contributions to genetic research, is also the director of the Human Genome Project. He eloquently melds human biology and religion:

> As the director of the Human Genome Project, I have led a consortium of scientists to read out the 3.1 billion letters of the human genome, our own DNA instruction book. As a believer, I see DNA, the information molecule of all living things, as God's language, and the elegance and complexity of our own bodies and the rest of nature as a reflection of God's plan. . . . Can you

both pursue an understanding of how life works using the tools of genetics and molecular biology, and worship a creator God? Aren't evolution and faith in God incompatible? Can a scientist believe in miracles like the resurrection? Actually, I find no conflict here, and neither apparently do the 40 percent of working scientists who claim to be believers . . . . I have found there is a wonderful harmony in the complementary truths of science and faith. The God of the Bible is also the God of the genome. God can be found in the cathedral or in the laboratory. By investigating God's majestic and awesome creation, science can actually be a means of worship. If the human genome can be viewed as the language of God, then human beings can be viewed as the consummate expression of that language . . . [154]

In the New Saint Joseph Sunday Missal, the Reverend John C. Kersten, S.V.D. comments on the moral component of debating controversial issues such as abortion:

Should controversy be avoided at any cost? It seems impossible to do so if one wants to go by values that are not negotiable in good conscience. The person who tries to be nice all the time usually ends up losing friends and incurs the serious troubles associated with constant compromising. If we stand for values like love, justice and truth, we are controversial and might even hurt feelings. Jesus Christ was controversial. A careful reading of the Gospels shows that he was in conflict with opponents all the time. Like our Lord, we Christians are supposed to be a light in our dim and confused human condition. But being honest in business and public office and advocating values like fidelity, justice, and truth must result in controversy every so often. We should have the courage to face it, and follow our conscience when it dictates action or requires an absolute 'no'.[155]

Chapter 13–Are you up for the challenge?

Faced with what is right, and not do it shows a lack of courage.- Confucius

What would life be if we had no courage to attempt anything?–Vincent van Gogh

The only thing necessary for the triumph of evil is for good men to do nothing. – Edmund Burke

The hottest places in hell are reserved for those who, in a period of crisis, maintain their neutrality.–Dante

Almost all of us, even many who believe in the sanctity of life, are responsible for this abomination, because we either have allowed ourselves to be duped into believing it is acceptable to kill human life, or we have not stood up to defend life and work toward changing hearts, minds, and laws. For almost 50 years, we tolerated abortion. For almost 50 years, we've looked the other way and done nothing. For almost 50 years, we've said "oh, how terrible", then went back to our daily lives and forgot about it. As Fr. Spitzer states:

The work we are doing to try to change legislation, get appeals in the courts are all good, but
if you do not have a population that feels the
indignation and the wrongness of abortion that
is going to back you up, it won't go anywhere. It's
the rubber-band problem. You might be able to
get a Ronald Reagan or George Bush to help you
out. But then you get Obama, and you are back to
square one. We need a critical mass of the population who can back these people into a corner
and keep the fight going — no matter who is in
office. So the solution is education. I want to do it
in a way that gets to the profound elements very
fast, very quickly.[156]

What can we do to stand up and stop this slaughter? The
first challenge is to move out of your comfort zone. Is it easy?
No, but would you rush to the toddler about to drink from
the bleach bottle after getting into the cabinet of household
cleaners? Then why not save an unborn life? Be a hero. You
don't have to write a book. You don't have to become a public
speaker. Becoming a hero can involve something as easy as
writing a letter to your congressional representative or taking
used maternity and baby clothes to your local crisis pregnancy
center. The difference between this and the example of the pre-
vious paragraph is that we almost never know how many lives
we save by becoming active in the pro-life movement. The following are some specific things you can do now to save lives.

1. Become politically charged. Not only vote pro-life, but
    make it clear to your representatives in Washington and
    your state capital that you do. Sending mail to pro-life
    politicians supporting their work will encourage them

to become even more committed to protecting innocent life. A continuous inundation of logical, fact-based arguments to your anti-life representatives will make clear to them they are on the wrong side of this crucial issue and that their days in Washington or your state capital are numbered.

2. Educate yourself on life issues, so that you can make the truth about abortion clear to friends, family, neighbors, co-workers, and anyone else. You have already started this step by having read this book this far. You will feel more confident about engaging others in conversation when the topic does come up, and can effectively argue the truth and dispel the hype, distortions, and lies, and have the courage to do so. However, this has been made more difficult due to one of our culture's most recent, popular, and socially required taboos: that one should never offer advice, input or an opinion regarding another's moral dilemmas and decisions. The *de rigueur* verbiage sounds something like this: "I'm not in favor of abortion, but I would never tell someone else what to do." In reality, it's not about "telling someone what to do", it's about bringing them back to a realization of truth, and caring enough about the person to save them from a disastrous decision that will have negative effects on her or him for the rest of her or his life. An interesting side note is that the mantra of never "telling someone what to do" seems to apply only to issues such as abortion. When was the last time we heard someone say, "I don't agree with him beating his dog, but I would never tell someone what to do."

3. Join, support financially, and become active in pro-life organizations. Fortunately, their number has been growing rapidly in the last five years. The following are only a few suggestions.

Live Action (lifeaction.org) Lead by Lila Rose, Life Action is one of the most active pro-life organizations.

Students for Life of America (https://studentsforlife. org) One of the newest and fasting growing pro-life groups in the U.S., working especially among high school and college students.

American Life League (www.all.org) is one of the nation's largest grassroots Catholic pro-life organizations.

Voices for Life (https://www.voices4life.org) is a group that works with pro-life youth.

Pro-Life Action League (https://prolifeaction.org)

Priests for Life (www.priestsforlife.org)

Human Coalition (www.humancoalition.org)

National Pro-Life Alliance (www.prolifealliance.com)

Care Net (www.care-net.org)

National Right to Life (www.nrlc.org) is the nation's oldest major pro-life organization. It has 50 state affiliates and more than 3,000 local chapters.

Noteworthy is the fact that for decades after Roe v. Wade, there were a handful of pro-life organizations. Today, there are so many, it's hard to keep up with them all, and the number is still growing. An internet search will yield dozens more pro-life organizations worth investigating and joining, many active at the state and local levels. The following is just a sampling: Democrats for Life of America, Feminists for Life, Libertarians for Life, Physicians for Life, Pro-Life Alliance of Gays and Lesbians, Republican National Coalition for Life, and Secular Pro-Life.

4. Step out in public: attend a 40 Days for Life prayer vigil outside a Planned Parenthood clinic. Abby Johnson revealed that when there is a peaceful pro-life presence outside a clinic, their "business" falls by as much as 75%. You can also participate in the annual nationwide walks or marches held in at least 87 cities and towns across the United States and the original and largest march in Washington D.C. For a complete list, visit https://march-forlife.org/ and click on "march against abortion in your home state".

5. Volunteer at a crisis pregnancy center. There are approximately 2,750 around the United States. Google search the one nearest you.

6. Stop buying products and services from businesses that directly or indirectly financially support Planned Parenthood, and write to them telling them the reason for your boycott. Get friends, family, neighbors and co-workers to do the same. For a complete list, visit https://familycouncil.org/?page_id=14547

7.   Loan this book to a friend, or buy them a copy, whether they are pro-life or anti-life, and request that they pass it along to another friend after reading it.

If every pro-life person in the country did just one of these things a month, spent at least 15 minutes a month in these pro-life activities, we could end abortion in the United States. Yes, we have busy lives, but we can find 15 minutes a month to be a hero. There is no greater satisfaction or excitement than knowing you have saved an innocent life. If you have been anti-life up to now, be honest, courageous, and open minded enough to consider an alternate viewpoint. Give your life meaning and purpose. Have conviction. Have courage. Step up. Now, more than ever, it's time.

BIBLIOGRAPHY

1. Abortion Statistics. American Life League. Accessed August 4, 2019. https://www.all.org/learn/abortion/abortion-statistics/

2. Induced Abortion in the United States. Guttmacher Institute. Published May 3, 2016. Accessed August 4, 2019. https://www.guttmacher.org/fact-sheet/induced-abortion-united-states

3. U.S. Abortion Statistics. Accessed August 4, 2019. https://abort73.com/abortion_facts/us_abortion_statistics

4. Planning O of P and. National Center for Veterans Analysis and Statistics. Accessed August 4, 2019. https://www.va.gov/vetdata/

5. Cancer Facts and Statistics | American Cancer Society. Accessed August 4, 2019. https://www.cancer.org/research/cancer-facts-statistics.html

6. Sedgh G. Legal Abortion Worldwide: Incidence and Recent Trends. *International Family Planning Perspectives*. 2007;33(3):11.

7. Planned Parenthood Is Wrong: Abortion Is Not Health Care. National Review. Published December 11, 2018. Accessed August 4, 2019. https://www.nationalreview.com/2018/12/planned-parenthood-calls-abortion-health-care/

8. Ekeocha O. *Target Africa: Ideological Neocolonialism in the Twenty-First Century*. Ignatius Press; 2018.

9. Am, October 7 apresto, 2016. Ben Shapiro DESTROYS Abortion Argument: "No More Euphemisms" | Daily Wire. Published October 7, 2016. Accessed August 4, 2019. /news/9768/ben-shapiro-destroys-abortion-argument-no-more-amanda-prestigiacomo

10. *Hollywood vs. America*. In: *Wikipedia*. ; 2019. Accessed August 4, 2019. https://en.wikipedia.org/w/index.php?title=Hollywood_vs._America&oldid=901811585

11. Newman L, Rowley J, Hoorn SV, et al. Global Estimates of the Prevalence and Incidence of Four Curable Sexually Transmitted Infections in 2012 Based on Systematic Review and Global Reporting. *PLOS ONE*. 2015;10(12):e0143304. doi:10.1371/journal.pone.0143304

12. Centers for Disease Control (CDC). Teenage pregnancy and fertility trends United States, 1974, 1980. *MMWR Morb Mortal Wkly Rep*. 1985;34(19):277-280.

13. March for Life (Washington, D.C.). In: *Wikipedia*. ; 2019. Accessed August 14, 2019. https://en.wikipedia.org/w/index.php?title=March_for_Life_(Washington,_D.C.)&oldid=907524769

14. New March for Life Video Celebrates Defenders of the Unborn. News Busters. Accessed August 14, 2019. https://www.newsbusters.org/blogs/katie-yoder/2015/01/22/new-march-life-video-celebrates-defenders-unborn

15. The Reason There's No "Official" Estimate of How Many People Will Be at the March for Life. The Blaze. Published January 22, 2015. Accessed August 14, 2019. https://www.

theblaze.com/news/2015/01/22/the-reason-theres-no-official-estimate-of-how-many-people-will-be-at-the-march-for-life

16. Gosnell, Grand Jury Report.pdf. Accessed August 14, 2019. https://cdn.cnsnews.com/documents/Gosnell,%20 Grand%20Jury%20Report.pdf

17. Philadelphia abortion clinic horror: Column. Accessed August 14, 2019. https://www.usa-today.com/story/opinion/2013/04/10/ philadelphia-abortion-clinic-horror-column/2072577/

18. Blackburn and Scalise Outraged by Media Cover-up of Planned Parenthood Scandal and Gosnell Murders. Congressman Steve Scalise. Published April 17, 2013. Accessed August 14, 2019. https://scalise.house.gov/ press-release/blackburn-and-scalise-outraged-media-cover-planned-parenthood-scandal-and-gosnell

19. Why Horrifying Abortion Clinic Was Not Inspected For 17 Years. HuffPost. Published 33:21 500. Accessed August 14, 2019. https://www.huffpost.com/entry/ kermit-gosnell-abortion-c_n_812702

20. The Media Elite. In: *Wikipedia.* ; 2019. Accessed August 14, 2019. https://en.wikipedia.org/w/index. php?title=The_Media_Elite&oldid=910815381

21. Ugarte R. Mass Communications and the 1976 Presidential Election. Items. Accessed October 19, 2019. https:// items.ssrc.org/from-our-archives/mass-communica-tions-and-the-1976-presidential-election/

22. Media Bias Basics. Accessed August 14, 2019. http://archive. mrc.org/biasbasics/biasbasics1.asp

23. Lichter SR, Noyes R. *Good Intentions Make Bad News: Why Americans Hate Campaign Journalism.* Rowman & Littlefield; 1996.

24. Lichter SR, Rothman S, Lichter LS. *The Media Elite.* Adler & Adler; 1986.

25. Soley LC. *The News Shapers: The Sources Who Explain the News.* Greenwood Publishing Group; 1992.

26. CENSORED! How Online Media Companies Are Suppressing Conservative Speech. Accessed August 15, 2019. https://www.newsbusters.org/blogs/culture/ashley-rae-goldenberg/2018/04/16/censored-how-online-media-companies-are-suppressing

27. Abortion Procedures: 1st, 2nd, and 3rd Trimesters "YouTube. Accessed August 15, 2019. https://www.youtube.com/watch?v=CFZDhM5Gwhk

28. Fetal development: MedlinePlus Medical Encyclopedia. Accessed August 15, 2019. https://medlineplus.gov/ency/article/002398.htm

29. Abortion: Get Facts About the Procedure and Statistics. EMedicineHealth. Accessed August 15, 2019. https://www.emedicinehealth.com/abortion/article_em.htm

30. Baby's "angelic" face haunts former abortion nurse. Baptist Press. Accessed August 15, 2019. http://www.bpnews.net/17012/babys-angelic-face-haunts-former-abortion-nurse

31. GONZALES v. CARHART. LII / Legal Information Institute. Accessed August 15, 2019. https://www.law.cornell.edu/supremecourt/text/05-380

32. "Partial-Birth Abortion": Separating Fact From Spin. NPR.org. Accessed August 17, 2019. https://www.npr.org/2006/02/21/5168163/partial-birth-abortion-separating-fact-from-spin

33. THE FITZSIMMONS &quotREVELATION". Washington Examiner. Published March 17, 1997. Accessed August 17, 2019. https://www.washingtonexaminer.com/weekly-standard/the-fitzsimmons-quotrevelation

34. Epner JEG, Jonas HS, Seckinger DL. Late-term Abortion. *JAMA*. 1998;280(8):724-729. doi:10.1001/jama.280.8.724

35. Inc G. Gallup Brain: Opinions on Partial-Birth Abortions. Gallup.com. Accessed August 17, 2019. https://news.gallup.com/poll/8791/Gallup-Brain-Opinions-PartialBirth-Abortions.aspx

36. News NRL. Nurse quits after witnessing abortion of a 4-pound baby girl. NRL News Today. Published May 13, 2015. Accessed August 17, 2019. https://www.national-righttolifenews.org/2015/05/nurse-quits-after-witness-ing-abortion-of-a-4-pound-baby-girl/

37. Hobbs J. 10 Numbers You Should Know About Pregnancy Centers. Accessed August 17, 2019. https://pregnancy-helpnews.com/phc-10-numbers

38. Hobbs J. Report: Pregnancy centers saved 300,000 babies from abortion in 2015. Live Action News. Published January 6, 2016. Accessed August 17, 2019. https://www.liveaction.org/news/pregnancy-care-centers-saved-300000-babies-from-abortion-in-2015/

39. What Women Considering Abortion Need. FemCatholic. Published November 29, 2018. Accessed

August 17, 2019. http://www.femcatholic.com/what-abortion-minded-women-need/

40. Kathleen Eaton Bravo | Educational Dessert 2018 "YouTube. Accessed August 17, 2019. https://www.youtube.com/watch?v=DXG9B2r55IA

41. Abby Johnson: ProWoman, ProChild, ProLife. Accessed August 17, 2019. https://www.facebook.com/abbyjohnsonprolife/posts/2415091635167562

42. "Impulse Society" blames hyper-capitalism for America's social ills. Los Angeles Times. Published September 14, 2014. Accessed August 17, 2019. https://www.latimes.com/business/la-fi-books-20140914-story.html

43. NY Legislature Passes Bill That Makes Declawing Cats Illegal. NBC New York. Accessed August 17, 2019. http://www.nbcnewyork.com/news/local/Declawing-Cats-May-be-Banned-in-New-York-509323751.html

44. 16 U.S. Code § 668 Bald and golden eagles. LII / Legal Information Institute. Accessed August 17, 2019. https://www.law.cornell.edu/uscode/text/16/668

45. 2020 poll: 77 percent of Democrats back socialism, but most voters don't. Washington Examiner. Published February 25, 2019. Accessed August 20, 2019. https://www.washington-examiner.com/washington-secrets/2020-poll-77-dems-back-socialism-but-most-voters-dont

46. Flowers C, News PD. Opinion: No room for pro-lifers in Democratic Party. Newsday. Accessed August 20, 2019. https://www.newsday.com/opinion/commentary/no-room-for-pro-lifers-in-democratic-party-1.13538260

47. Catholicsentinel.org. Accessed August 20, 2019. https://catholicsentinel.org/Content/Social/Social/Article/Gov-Cuomo-says-New-York-has-no-room-for-extreme-conservatives-/-2/-2/23759

48. Israel M. The Necessity of the Born-Alive Abortion Survivors Protection Act. (4939):5.

49. Knights of Columbus-Marist Polls. Accessed August 18, 2019. http://www.kofc.org/en/news/polls.html#/

50. Questions and Answers on Late-Term Abortion | Charlotte Lozier Institute. Accessed August 18, 2019. https://lozierinstitute.org/questions-and-answers-on-late-term-abortion/

51. NW 1615 L. St, Washington S 800, Inquiries D 20036 U-419-4300 | M-419-4349 | F-419-4372 | M. Support for Abortion Slips. Pew Research Center's Religion & Public Life Project. Published October 1, 2009. Accessed August 18, 2019. https://www.pewforum.org/2009/10/01/support-for-abortion-slips/

52. Inc G. Abortion. Gallup.com. Accessed August 18, 2019. https://news.gallup.com/poll/1576/Abortion.aspx

53. Gallup poll shows more pro-lifers than pro-choicers. Accessed August 20, 2019. https://www.christianpost.com/voice/gallup-poll-shows-more-pro-lifers-than-pro-choicers.html

54. MORE SIGNS OF A PRO. Accessed August 20, 2019. https://www.nrlc.org/archive/news/2003/NRL07/more_signs_of_a_pro.htm

55. Reasons U.S. Women Have Abortions: Quantitative and Qualitative Perspectives. Guttmacher Institute. Published September 6, 2005. Accessed August 20, 2019. https://www.

guttmacher.org/journals/psrh/2005/reasons-us-women-have-abortions-quantitative-and-qualitative-perspectives

56. Millennials will change abortion conversation: Column. Accessed August 20, 2019. https://www.usatoday.com/story/opinion/2015/03/23/abortion-generation-demographics-choice-life-column/24900705/

57. Euthanasia in the Netherlands. Alliance VITA. Published November 24, 2017. Accessed May 3, 2020. https://www.alliancevita.org/en/2017/11/euthanasia-in-the-netherlands/

58. Dutch to prosecute doctor who euthanized woman with dementia. AP NEWS. Published November 9, 2018. Accessed May 3, 2020. https://apnews.com/15805d9d1d4345dab2a657f26697a775

59. Toolis K. The most dangerous man in the world. *The Guardian*. https://www.theguardian.com/lifeandstyle/1999/nov/06/weekend.kevintoolis. Published November 6, 1999. Accessed May 3, 2020.

60. Giubilini A, Minerva F. After-birth abortion: Why should the baby live? *Journal of Medical Ethics*. 2013;39(5):261-263. doi:10.1136/medethics-2011-100411

61. Infanticide is Not a Human Right. National Catholic Register. Accessed May 3, 2020. https://www.ncregister.com/blog/astagnaro/infanticide-is-not-a-human-right

62. The Corruption of the Science of Human Embryology | Physicians for Life. Accessed August 27, 2019. http://www.physiciansforlife.org/the-corruption-of-the-science-of-human-embryology/

63. User S. When Do Human Beings Begin? Accessed August 27, 2019. https://www.catholiceducation.org/en/controversy/abortion/when-do-human-beings-begin.html

64. When Do Human Beings Begin? Accessed August 27, 2019. https://www.princeton.edu/~prolife/articles/wdhbb.html

65. Why Life Begins At Conception. NAAPC. Accessed August 27, 2019. https://naapc.org/why-life-begins-at-conception/

66. News NRL. Abortionist: My career is "emotionally satisfying." NRL News Today. Published July 7, 2014. Accessed August 27, 2019. https://www.nationalrighttolifenews.org/2014/07/abortionist-my-career-is-emotionally-satisfying/

67. Fetal Surgery In UteroMedical Clinical Policy Bulletins | Aetna. Accessed August 17, 2019. http://www.aetna.com/cpb/medical/data/400_499/0449.html

68. 3711005.pdf. Accessed August 28, 2019. https://www.guttmacher.org/sites/default/files/pdfs/pubs/psrh/full/3711005.pdf

69. American AdoptionsHow Many Couples Are Waiting to Adopt? Accessed August 28, 2019. https://www.americanadoptions.com/pregnant/waiting_adoptive_families

70. Pregnancy-Related Deaths Happen Before, During, and Up to a Year After Delivery | CDC Online Newsroom | CDC. Published May 14, 2019. Accessed August 28, 2019. https://www.cdc.gov/media/releases/2019/p0507-pregnancy-related-deaths.html

71. O'Brien C. Forum in Dublin on maternal health. The Irish Times. Accessed August 28, 2019. https://www.irishtimes.com/news/forum-in-dublin-on-maternal-health-1.527381

72. Organisation mondiale de la santé, Fonds des Nations Unies pour l'enfance, Fonds des Nations unies pour la population, Banque internationale pour la reconstruction et le développement. *Maternal Mortality in 2005 Estimates Developed by WHO, UNICEF, UNFPA and The World Bank.* World Health Organization; 2008.

73. Supreme Mistakes: Legal scholars pick five worst U.S. Supreme Court rulings > Washtenaw County Legal News. Accessed August 28, 2019. http://www.legalnews.com/washtenaw/947577

74. Calderone MS. Illegal Abortion as a Public Health Problem. *Am J Public Health Nations Health.* 1960;50(7):948-954. doi:10.2105/AJPH.50.7.948

75. The Best Pro-Life Arguments for Secular Audiences. Accessed August 28, 2019. https://www.frc.org/brochure/the-best-pro-life-arguments-for-secular-audiences

76. Novielli C. Planned Parenthood debunked: No, thousands of women didn't die yearly from abortion before Roe. Live Action News. Published March 9, 2019. Accessed August 28, 2019. https://www.liveaction.org/news/planned-parenthood-debunked-thousands-abortion-die/

77. Balan M. Liberal Kristof Admits Conservatives More Generous Than Liberals. Media Research Center. Published December 22, 2008. Accessed August 31, 2019. https://www.mrc.org/articles/liberal-kristof-admits-conservatives-more-generous-liberals

78. Who Really Cares? National Review. Published November 28, 2006. Accessed August 31, 2019. https://www.nationalreview.com/2006/11/who-really-cares-thomas-sowell/

79. Why the States Did Not Prosecute Women for Abortion Before Roe v. Wade. Americans United for Life. Published April 23, 2010. Accessed September 2, 2019. https://aul.org/2010/04/23/why-the-states-did-not-prosecute-women-for-abortion-before-roe-v-wade/

80. Are we losing a sense of what it means to be human? | OC Catholic. Accessed September 2, 2019. https://occatholic.com/are-we-losing-a-sense-of-what-it-means-to-be-human/

81. Abortion and Down Syndrome. Healthline. Accessed September 2, 2019. https://www.healthline.com/health-news/the-debate-over-terminating-down-syndrome-pregnancies

82. Bureau UC. Section 2. Births, Deaths, Marriages, and Divorces. Accessed September 2, 2019. https://www.census.gov/library/publications/2011/compendia/statab/131ed/births-deaths-marriages-divorces.html

83. Cancer Facts and Statistics | American Cancer Society. Accessed September 2, 2019. https://www.cancer.org/research/cancer-facts-statistics.html

84. Additional Resources|Suicide|Violence Prevention|Injury Center|CDC. Published July 26, 2019. Accessed September 2, 2019. https://www.cdc.gov/violenceprevention/suicide/resources.html

85. Fetal development: MedlinePlus Medical Encyclopedia. Accessed September 2, 2019. https://medlineplus.gov/ency/article/002398.htm

86. Abby Johnson Kentucky Senate Testimony February 14, 2019YouTube. Accessed September 2, 2019. https://www.youtube.com/watch?v=zj7S75Dp3GQ

87. Gonzaga Faith & Reason Institute | Gonzaga University. Accessed September 7, 2019. https://www.gonzaga.edu/academics/gonzaga-faith-reason-institute

88. Father Spitzer's 10 Universal Principles. National Catholic Register. Accessed September 7, 2019. http://www.ncregister.com/daily-news/father-spitzers-10-universal-principles

89. User S. Introduction and Principles of Ethics. Accessed September 7, 2019. https://www.catholiceducation.org/en/religion-and-philosophy/philosophy/introduction-amp-principles-of-ethics.html

90. Just-the-facts-ten-principles1.pdf. Accessed September 7, 2019. https://c4oh.files.wordpress.com/2012/07/just-the-facts-ten-principles1.pdf

91. Ten Universal Principles. Accessed September 7, 2019. https://www.ignatius.com/Ten-Universal-Principles-P2509.aspx

92. FindLaw's United States Supreme Court case and opinions. Findlaw. Accessed September 7, 2019. https://caselaw.findlaw.com/us-supreme-court/60/393.html

93. Roe v. Wade. LII / Legal Information Institute. Accessed September 7, 2019. https://www.law.cornell.edu/supremecourt/text/410/113

94. Freiburger C. Article in Harvard Law Journal concludes: The preborn child is a constitutional person. Live Action News. Published June 1, 2017. Accessed September 7, 2019. https://www.liveaction.org/news/landmark-harvard-essay-preborn-child-constitutional-person/

95. The Best Pro-Life Arguments for Secular Audiences. Accessed September 7, 2019. https://www.frc.org/brochure/the-best-pro-life-arguments-for-secular-audiences

96. Ely JH. The Wages of Crying Wolf: A Comment on Roe v. Wade. :31.

97. The Lingering Problems With *roe V. Wade*, And Why The Recent Senate Hearings On Michael Mcconnell's Nomination Only Underlined Them. Findlaw. Accessed September 7, 2019. https://supreme.findlaw.com/legal-commentary/the-lingering-problems-with-roe-v-wade-and-why-the-recent-senate-hearings-on-michael-mcconnells-nomination-only-underlined-them.html

98. Wittes B. Letting Go of Roe. The Atlantic. Published January 1, 2005. Accessed September 7, 2019. https://www.theatlantic.com/magazine/archive/2005/01/letting-go-of-roe/303695/

99. Ginsburg RB. Some Thoughts on Autonomy and Equality in Relation to Roe v. Wade. *NORTH CAROLINA LAW REVIEW*. 63:13.

100. Gluck AR, Metzger G. A Conversation with Justice Ruth Bader Ginsburg. :25.

101. Chicago Tribune from Chicago, Illinois on March 5, 1997 · Page 99. Newspapers.com. Accessed September 7, 2019. http://www.newspapers.com/newspage/168718786/

102. Terzo S. 7 powerful quotes from "Jane Roe" of Roe v. Wade. Live Action News. Published January 20, 2016. Accessed September 7, 2019. https://www.liveaction.org/news/7-powerful-quotes-from-jane-roe-of-roe-v-wade/

103. Israel M. Planned Parenthood's Annual Report Is Out. Here's What You Need to Know. The Heritage Foundation. Accessed October 27, 2019. https://www.heritage.org/life/ commentary/planned-parenthoods-annual-report-out-heres-what-you-need-know

104. 190118-annualreport18-p01.pdf. Accessed October 28, 2019. https://www.plannedparenthood.org/uploads/filer_ public/80/d7/80d7d7c7-977c-4036-9c61-b3801741b441 /190118-annualreport18-p01.pdf

105. Peck B. 6 Things to Know from Planned Parenthood's Annual Report. March For Life. Published May 31, 2017. Accessed September 7, 2019. https://marchforlife.org/ pp-latest-report/

106. Definition of healthcare | Dictionary.com. Www.dictionary. com. Accessed September 7, 2019. https://www.dictionary. com/browse/healthcare

107. Dictionary by Merriam-Webster: America's most-trusted online dictionary. Accessed September 7, 2019. https:// www.merriam-webster.com/

108. Planned_Parenthood_Services.pdf. Accessed September 8, 2019. https://www.plannedparenthood.org/ files/4013/9611/7243/Planned_Parenthood_Services.pdf

109. PlannedParenthoodNumbers.pdf. Accessed May 3, 2020. http://www.adfmedia.org/files/ PlannedParenthoodNumbers.pdf

110. Plannedparenthoodnumbers.pdf. Accessed September 8, 2019. http://www.adfmedia.org/files/plannedparent-hoodnumbers.pdf

111. The 3% Myth | Live Action. Accessed September 8, 2019. https://www.liveaction.org/learn/3percent/

112. Parental Consent & Notification Laws | Teen Abortion Laws. Accessed September 8, 2019. https://www.planned-parenthood.org/learn/teens/preventing-pregnancy-stds/parental-consent-and-notification-laws

113. Life Collaborative of Middlesex County. Accessed October 26, 2019. https://www.facebook.com/permalink.php?story_fbid=373191566929750&id=258843645081210

114. Talking Sex, Puberty & Relationships: A Resource for Parents. Accessed September 8, 2019. https://www.plannedparenthood.org/learn/parents

115. Debunking Planned Parenthood's "3%" Abortion myth YouTube. Accessed September 10, 2019. https://www.youtube.com/watch?v=qtgqxvaV-8U

116. SHOCK VIDEO: Abortionist Says "I Have to Hit the Gym" to Build Strength for Dismemberment Abortions. CBN News. Published March 29, 2017. Accessed October 29, 2019. https://www1.cbn.com/cbnnews/us/2017/march/i-have-to-hit-the-gym-says-abortionist-of-strength-needed-to-perform-dismemberment-abortions

117. http://www.washingtontimes.com TWT. Video: Planned Parenthood exec who 'wanted a Lamborghini' caught haggling over baby body parts. The Washington Times. Accessed October 29, 2019. https://www.washingtontimes.com/news/2017/apr/26/planned-parenthood-executive-who-wanted-lamborghin/

118. Second Planned Parenthood Senior Executive Haggles Over Baby Parts Prices, Changes Abortion Methods YouTube.

Accessed September 10, 2019. https://www.youtube.com/watch?v=MjCs_gvImyw

119. Charges Dropped Against Activists Who Exposed Planned Parenthood's Baby Body Parts Scandal. Accessed September 10, 2019. https://www.christianpost.com/news/judge-dismisses-felony-charges-against-pro-life-planned-parenthood-video-activist-david-daleiden.html

120. Houston Prosecutor "Colluding" With Planned Parenthood to Indict David Daleiden, Lawyers Says. Accessed September 10, 2019. https://www.christianpost.com/news/houston-prosecutor-colluding-planned-parenthood-indict-david-daleiden.html

121. *David Daleiden on Kamala Harris and Planned Parenthood.*; 2019. Accessed September 10, 2019. https://www.youtube.com/watch?v=fMjtYHakXxM

122. Fl N, ers. Court testimony: Consultant said finding abortionist who risks born-alive infants best way to get body parts. Live Action News. Published October 24, 2019. Accessed October 24, 2019. https://www.liveaction.org/news/court-abortion-consultant-abortionist-born-alive-body/

123. Human Capital–Episode 3: Planned Parenthood's Custom Abortions for Superior Product. The Center for Medical Progress. Published August 19, 2015. Accessed October 24, 2019. https://www.centerformedicalprogress.org/2015/08/human-capital-episode-3-planned-parenthoods-custom-abortions-for-superior-product/

124. Rousselle C. Did Planned Parenthood cover up child abuse and sex trafficking? Catholic News Agency. Accessed October 26, 2019. https://www.catholicnewsagency.com/

news/did-planned-parenthood-cover-up-child-sex-trafficking-and-abuse-10771/

125. http://www.washingtontimes.com TWT. Planned Parenthood failed to take sex trafficking seriously after infamous sting, ex-employee says. The Washington Times. Accessed October 26, 2019. https://www.washingtontimes.com/news/2017/jan/17/planned-parenthood-failed-take-sex-trafficking-ser/

126. Abortion A Liberal Cause? (Margaret Sanger and Eugenics). Accessed October 10, 2019. http://groups.csail.mit.edu/mac/users/rauch/abortion_eugenics/peterson.html

127. Margaret Sanger (Ft. Clarence J. Gamble & Jean Baker) – Letter from Margaret Sanger to Dr. C.J. Gamble. Genius. Accessed October 10, 2019. https://genius.com/Margaret-sanger-letter-from-margaret-sanger-to-dr-cj-gamble-annotated

128. The Public Papers of Margaret Sanger: Web Edition. Accessed October 11, 2019. https://www.nyu.edu/projects/sanger/webedition/app/documents/show.php?sangerDoc=129037.xml

129. The Pivot of Civilization, by Margaret Sanger. Accessed October 11, 2019. https://www.gutenberg.org/files/1689/1689-h/1689-h.htm

130. The Project Gutenberg eBook of Margaret Sanger an Autobiography. Accessed October 11, 2019. http://www.gutenberg.org/files/56610/56610-h/56610-h.htm

131. estherkatz. Sanger and Mike Wallace. Margaret Sanger Papers Project. Published April 11, 2012. Accessed

October 11, 2019. https://sangerpapers.wordpress.com/2012/04/11/sanger-and-mike-wallace/

132. Yeh B. 7 shocking quotes by Planned Parenthood's founder. Live Action News. Published February 21, 2015. Accessed October 11, 2019. https://www.liveaction.org/news/7-shocking-quotes-by-planned-parenthoods-founder/

133. Margaret Sanger Quotes, History, and Biography "Research, Statistics, and Abortion History. Research, Statistics, and History on Abortion & Human Rights. Accessed October 11, 2019. https://www.liveaction.org/research/margaret-sanger-quotes-history-and-biography/

134. *Bishop Barron on Shocking Abortion Numbers.* Accessed October 11, 2019. https://www.youtube.com/watch?v=sski0eebAAo

135. Wolf N. OUR BODIES, OUR SOULS. :8.

136. EDT KDO 4/20/10 at 4:55 P. Remember Roe? Young Activists Say They've Never Forgotten. Newsweek. Published April 20, 2010. Accessed October 11, 2019. https://www.newsweek.com/remember-roe-young-activists-say-theyve-never-forgotten-222722

137. Lewin T. Legal Abortion Under Fierce Attack 15 Years After Roe v. Wade Ruling. *The New York Times.* https://www.nytimes.com/1988/05/10/us/legal-abortion-under-fierce-attack-15-years-after-roe-v-wade-ruling.html. Published May 10, 1988. Accessed October 11, 2019.

138. Elizabeth Cady Stanton. *The Revolution–April 9, 1868.*; 1868. Accessed October 11, 2019. http://archive.org/details/revolution-1868-04-09

139. The Revolution, July 8 1869 – National Susan B. Anthony Museum & House. Accessed October 11, 2019. https://susan-banthonyhouse.org/blog/the-revolution-july-8-1869/

140. Eleven Thousand Reasons Why Planned Parenthood Can't Be Trusted. Default. Accessed October 11, 2019. https://www.adflegal.org/detailspages/blog-details/alli-anceedge/2017/10/18/eleven-thousand-reasons-why-planned-parenthood-can-t-be-trusted

141. ABORTION LIES AND OTHER SHADINGS OF THE TRUTH– Chicago Tribune. Accessed October 11, 2019. https://www.chicagotribune.com/news/ct-xpm-1997-03-05-9703050008-story.html

142. Everyone Needs to Repent for Tolerating Racism, Including Those Who Support Planned Parenthood "Standard Newswire. Accessed October 11, 2019. http://www.stan-dardnewswire.com/news/864465388.html

143. Pro Life "Anti Abortion Facts and Pro-Life Arguments. Accessed October 11, 2019. https://www.priestsforlife.org/library/index.aspx?lib=5

144. Judge Deals Blow To Texas Abortion Policy After Governor Declares It 'Non-Essential.' The Daily Wire. Accessed March 30, 2020. https://www.dailywire.com/news/judge-deals-blow-to-texas-abortion-policy-after-governor-declares-it-non-essential

145. Studnicki J. Late-Term Abortion and Medical Necessity: A Failure of Science. *Health Serv Res Manag Epidemiol.* 2019;6. doi:10.1177/2333392819841781

146. Miller DV. National Vital Statistics Reports, Volume 59, Number 1, (December 8, 2010). :72.

147. United States abortion rates, 1960-2013. Accessed October 11, 2019. http://www.johnstonsarchive.net/policy/abortion/graphusabrate.html

148. Undeniable-2017.pdf. Accessed October 12, 2019. https://firstliberty.org/wp-content/uploads/2017/05/Undeniable-2017.pdf

149. Reid M. SPUC Home. SPUC. Accessed October 12, 2019. https://www.spuc.org.uk/

150. Lanier G. Abortion in the Scrolls and the Didache. Greg Lanier. Published January 26, 2014. Accessed October 12, 2019. https://glanier.wordpress.com/2014/01/26/abortion-in-the-scrolls-and-the-didache/

151. Arguments Against Abortion. Accessed October 12, 2019. http://www.leaderu.com/orgs/probe/docs/arg-abor.html

152. NW 1615 L. St, Washington S 800, Inquiries D 20036 U-419-4300 | M-419-4349 | F-419-4372 | M. Public Opinion on Abortion. Pew Research Center's Religion & Public Life Project. Accessed October 12, 2019. https://www.pewforum.org/fact-sheet/public-opinion-on-abortion/

153. NW 1615 L. St, Suite 800Washington, Inquiries D 20036USA202-419-4300 | M-857-8562 | F-419-4372 | M. Key takeaways about Latino voters in the 2018 midterm elections. Pew Research Center. Accessed October 12, 2019. https://www.pewresearch.org/fact-tank/2018/11/09/how-latinos-voted-in-2018-midterms/

154. The-language-of-god-_-A-scientist-presents-evidence-for-belief-by-francis-s.-collins.pdf. Accessed October 12, 2019. https://www.difa3iat.com/wp-content/uploads/2014/06/

The-language-of-god-_-A-scientist-presents-evidence-for-belief-by-francis-s.-collins.pdf

155. Church C. *New St. Joseph Sunday Missal: The Complete Masses for Sundays, Holydays, and the Easter Triduum ; Mass Themes and Biblical Commentaries by John C. Kersten.* Catholic Book Publishing Company; 1999.

156. Father Spitzer's 10 Universal Principles. National Catholic Register. Accessed October 12, 2019. http://www.ncregister.com/daily-news/father-spitzers-10-universal-principles